THE Frailty OF A Butterfly

MY JOURNEY THROUGH NEWBORN LOSS

Mary Wasacz

The Frailty of a Butterfly

My Journey Through Newborn Loss

Mary Wasacz

ISBN: 978-1-66789-171-2

DEDICATION

This book is dedicated in memory of John Driscoll, JR., M.D.
for the care of our newborn, Cathy Anne, and us
in the most challenging time of our lives. He will
always have a special place in our hearts.

In memory of

Cathy Anne Wasacz

July 17, 1977 - August 16,1977

CHAPTER 1, JULY 17, 1977

... this is my baby grasping for life, not a movie or fiction

The nurse rolls me into a large, stark white room. There is an instrument tray to the left, which is draped with a sterile towel. I manage to transfer onto the delivery table from the stretcher in-between contractions. John, my husband, is at my side. I'm happy he's with me to greet our baby as he did for our other two children. I find pushing hard, but after one long push, the baby pops out.

"Hello, beautiful girl," says John. He beams from ear to ear and looks adoringly at me as he gives me a gentle kiss on the forehead.

Immediately the doctor hands Cathy Anne to me. She is so much like three-year old Mary Christina with her round face and chubby cheeks but within seconds, right before my eyes, her features change. Her cheeks sink. The muscles of her face have relaxed. It is frightening seeing her so flaccid, like a rag doll. She is ashen in color with almond-shaped eyes, her neck fans out like a web. She holds her fingers in a fixed position and her ears seem low. I don't know what is wrong. She's not breathing, is turning blue, and doesn't cry.

"Please, God, please, help her. Why doesn't she breathe?" I say out loud. "Dear God, help her breathe. Dear God, please take care of our little baby. Hail Mary, full of grace …"

1

The doctor cuts the cord, takes her from me, and walks to the other side of the room to give her oxygen via a mask over her nose and mouth. It takes about ten minutes. It seems like hours before she is breathing on her own. I feel like I'm in a black hole, and there's no way out. Frantic. Thoughts race through my head. I'm unable to utter anything to John. *What is wrong with her? Is it fatal? Does she have brain damage?*

"Mary, I think our prayers must've convinced God to let her stay with us," says John. The nurse and doctor are in the room, but no one says anything.

I fear our new baby will die and there is nothing I, a registered nurse myself, can do. I clap my hands to see if she will respond, hoping to cause the startle or Moro reflex, an involuntary response indicating a normal, developing nervous system in a newborn. She doesn't respond. I have high anxiety, a fluttering in my stomach and a tightness in my chest. The obstetrician doesn't say anything about her condition and I don't ask. I don't know what to ask. I know from experience as a nurse in labor and delivery, which I also taught in a nursing school, that she will need further testing.

I had wanted to stay home as long as possible while in labor, to walk around the garden and be with our children instead of being stuck in bed as a patient in the hospital.

"It's a good thing we came to the hospital. Thanks to you, John. We were only here fifteen minutes before she was born."

"Wow, thank God. She would've died if she wasn't born here," says John.

"Glad our wonderful doctor didn't have you step outside when she wasn't breathing. That's typical of doctors when something goes wrong. I can't imagine being here without you. I'll always be grateful to him."

I'm not tired because I had a delightful, relaxing day in the garden with John and our children. John and I had talked about our new baby, taking trips to visit friends, walks in the park—the children will push the carriage, go to activities at the pool. What a fun time we plan with our new addition.

The nurse takes Cathy Anne out of the delivery room to weigh her. Our baby is gone from our sight and I don't know what will become of her or what is happening to her. John and I are silent. I can feel strength coming from John's hands that I grasp in mine. The doctor and nurse leave the room without saying anything. I'm still in the delivery room when our pediatrician arrives.

"I ordered an x-ray. Her heart and lungs seem to be okay. She weighs 6 pounds 8 ounces and is 18 inches long."

"She's my smallest baby. I took vitamins. Could vitamins have caused her problem?" My mind is racing. I'm desperate to know if I've done something wrong.

"No."

"I didn't take vitamins with Johnny and Mary Christina. They were fine and weighed more at birth." The obstetrician I had for Mary Christina and Johnny's birth didn't believe in vitamins. He died from cancer shortly before this pregnancy. My obstetrician for this pregnancy prescribed vitamins. "Are you sure vitamins wouldn't have caused this?"

"Yes. Definitely. Vitamins wouldn't have caused it. I'll be back tomorrow." His manner is matter of fact and unflustered. My stomach is jumping up and down and my heart is beating faster.

I'm near tears. I wonder what's wrong with her. This can't be. I hope this is a nightmare and I'll wake up and our baby will be healthy.

"I have confidence in what the pediatrician will recommend for her. I'm nervous," I tell John. "But I'll try to stay calm. My stomach is jumping up and down." *Good thing I had that two-hour nap after dinner. No wonder I'm wide-awake.*

The truth is that I am worried about brain damage. Cathy Anne's ashen face keeps popping into my mind. I think I saw other abnormal traits. This is a horror and I know that all I can do is wait and pray. Strangely, I have no desire to touch or hold her. It is like watching a movie unfold where something suspenseful is about to occur. But this is my baby grasping for life, not a movie or piece of fiction.

CHAPTER 2

A monarch butterfly landed on my chest this morning

"You might as well go home. Nothing can be done tonight," I tell John. It's late, already 9:45 PM. "Please pray with my mother we'll have the strength to cope and get through this together." I was overcome with racing thoughts of what was going to happen to Cathy Anne. Would she live long? Does she have brain damage? What could possibly be her diagnosis?

"There's no point worrying till we know what's wrong, so put her in God's hands. He'll take care of her and us," says John. We kiss goodbye. I'm torn to tell John to leave, even though I would like him to be with me. I also need him to go home to tell my mother Cathy Anne isn't healthy. She's waiting to know the outcome of the birth. I know she's worried. My mother will be a good support and will pray with John. She always knows what to say. My mother is always kind to everybody and is nonjudgmental. She is a wonderful role model.

I'm transferred to the maternity room. I can't sleep. I still feel wide-awake. I do not cry. I am not emotional. Detached. I feel so perplexed by the outcome of Cathy Anne's birth. If only I had some warning that something was wrong during my pregnancy. But what could have prepared me for this? My anxiety is high, my stomach continues to flutter. I wish it would calm down.

I am alone in the maternity unit room, which gives me a lot of time to think when a nurse passes by my room. Nursing was the career I chose after I made a novena to the Blessed Mother asking for her intercession choosing my career. I chose psychiatric nursing as my profession, wanting to help patients with mental illness who were stigmatized in our society.

I trust God that He will take care of us no matter what the outcome. How could I have no idea Cathy Anne had any medical problems? She was a very active baby in utero; there was no reason to suspect anything was wrong. Perhaps that was good. I enjoyed my pregnancy and had no worries.

My mind shifts to this morning when I had sporadic, mild contractions. I spent the day in the garden, enjoying all the beauty of nature. As I was sitting in the garden, a monarch butterfly landed on my chest. The butterfly is the Christian symbol of the Resurrection and new life, the Christian belief of life after death, giving consolation and hope. The colorful markings of black stripes on its orange wings were striking, which made me think how unique our baby must be. How unusual for my baby in utero to be so close to this alluring winged creature. Little did I know how special she would be. I knew I would buy a figurine of a butterfly, in honor of Cathy Anne's birth, and put it on the table with Mary Christina's and Johnny's pictures.

Thoughts continue to race through my head. I find it difficult to concentrate. My anxiety continues to be high. I wish I could calm down. It's so hard not knowing what Cathy Anne's problem is. I hope it's something that can be fixed, but I'm fearful she has some fatal syndrome. I have never seen a baby with her traits. Her color shocked me.

There is such a need to know what to blame the condition on, to take chaos out of this situation. Did the vitamins cause Cathy Anne's problem? My pediatrician had said, "No." But I still wonder.

I have a flashback to the time I had a miscarriage early in our marriage. The feelings of doom I had then are the same feelings I am experiencing with Cathy Anne now. Much good came from our heartache of the miscarriage. John was supportive and loving which helped me heal. John wanted no part of Lamaze (prepared childbirth) which I believed in from my experiences in labor and delivery as an RN and as an instructor in a nursing school. I saw how essential the father was to the mother's welfare. After the miscarriage, he knew he wanted to be with me in the labor and delivery room.

My mother always said, "Out of tragedy, something good will come." What good will come from Cathy Anne's suffering and ours? Suffering is part of the human condition. Offering my suffering to God and uniting my suffering to Christ's suffering on the cross will help.

I pray Cathy Anne will have a positive effect on my children's lives. How will we manage? Prayer. The children were looking forward to being a big brother and a big sister. They practiced changing their dolls and stuffed animals in diapers so they could help in Cathy Anne's care. They helped me take the clothes which we washed for her out of the dryer. Johnny was so excited, jumped up and down when he saw his Winnie-the-Pooh blanket that Cathy Anne would use. My heart is broken for them.

Then my kitchen renovation snaps into my head. I think of the kitchen and all the work that is ahead and what a mess it is and how sad that I thought I'd be able to handle the renovation easily with a newborn because I never imagined that the baby wouldn't be perfectly healthy.

A new mother, Lizzie, is brought into my room. We talk all night, keeping my mind off fears of what will happen to Cathy Anne.

"How many children do you have?" I ask.

"This is my third. How about you? "

"My third also. Johnny's five, Mary Christina's three and this baby's a girl."

"I have two boys and just had a girl. I am so excited to finally have a girl! My oldest son was conceived in Japan. So, we say he was 'Made in Japan.' This makes us both chuckle.

"What were you doing in Japan?" I inquire.

"My husband's job. He's an engineer and head of a company."

"What does your husband do?" asks Lizzie.

"John teaches organic chemistry at Manhattan College. This summer he is doing a National Science Foundation postdoctoral fellowship at Columbia University. He'll be doing it for the next three summers."

After some more small talk, our conversation dies out and Lizzie falls asleep. I cannot sleep and think about how fortunate I am to have John as my husband.

The first time I met John was in October 1969 at a St. John's University Alumni dance. I feel fortunate we met each other because neither of us were planning on going. My good friend Ellen convinced me to go with her.

John was recovering from a broken collarbone. He broke it playing softball with his students at Manhattan College. The afternoon of the dance, the brace was finally taken off, otherwise he would not have gone. He felt like he looked like the Hunchback of Notre Dame. He took me home that evening and we dated every weekend. Three months later, in January 1970, he asked me to marry him. In his proposal he said, "I'd like to give you a ring." I wasn't sure if he meant a phone call or jewelry. We have many good laughs over that one. He always insists he meant a phone call. Our wedding was a magnificent winter day with the sun shining down on us from a clear blue sky. A crisp chill in the December air was a reminder of the snowstorm two days before. We were grateful the snow had stopped for our special day and not one of our 175 guests missed our new beginning.

We had so much fun going to parties, plays, movies, and concerts. Our life was wonderful, happy, and easy. What is in store for us with the birth of our third child? How will we cope with this child? Will life remain wonderful, happy, and easy?

The next morning Lizzie and I decide to visit the nursery to see our babies. There is such a difference in color between my baby and hers. Her baby has a beautiful pink color to her skin. Cathy Anne is ashen gray. There is another baby in the incubator next to Cathy Anne who also has a beautiful pink color. This baby's parents were in the Lamaze class I taught. It is upsetting to see the gray color of my baby's skin, a stark contrast to the other babies. I am left with an empty feeling, my heart broken in half, which I sit with. I continue to pray that John and I will have the strength from God to cope with whatever happens to her.

My pediatrician comes into my room and says, "I think Cathy Anne should be transferred to a New York City hospital where they have a neonatal unit and diagnostic tests not available here." He gives his opinion about the available hospitals. We chose the hospital he thought best for her needs.

"I had a student this last semester at Pace University that presented her neonatal unit at that hospital," I told him. I am comfortable sending her there because I know something about the unit and what the hospital has to offer. I feel God prepared us for this chapter in our life.

Ironically, our other two children were born in New York City. Here we are in Westchester, close to home, and have to move her to New York City, which is miles away. How unfair life is. I am so upset but know I have to do what is best for her.

CHAPTER 3

As Mary Christina is leaving, she gives me a big hug and a kiss

"**N**urse, I'd like Cathy Anne baptized before going to the City."

"Oh sure, I'll call the rectory."

After ten minutes, the nurse calls saying, "The priest is here, come to the nursery."

I walk into the nursery. I can feel my heart beating faster and faster, my stomach jumping up and down. There are no other babies in this room, which is fairly small. Cathy Anne, looking tiny and helpless, is in an isolette to the left of the room. There are windows above her letting sunlight flow in. Her ashen color hits me again—SMACK—in the face. My stomach sinks. A profound sadness hovers over the room. I look at her wondering what is going to become of her.

The priest pours holy water over Cathy Anne's head while pronouncing the words, "I baptize you in the name of the Father, and of the Son, and of the Holy Spirit." It never occurred to me to touch or hold her during her baptism. I wish someone would have suggested that.

Johnny, Mary Christina and my mother look inside the nursery window. What I didn't know at the time was that the nurse closed the curtains and my family was deprived of witnessing her baptism. I think the nurse was afraid of my children seeing their sick baby sister.

Baptism is the first sacrament of initiation into the Catholic faith community. I wanted Cathy Anne to be part of my faith, which I grew up in. Baptism is important to me because it welcomes her into the Catholic church and makes her a child of God.

"Thank you, Father, for coming." He smiles and says, "I will be praying for Cathy Anne and you and your family."

When I come out of the nursery, Mary Christina asks, "Why did the nurse close the curtains so I couldn't see Cathy Anne being baptized?"

"I'm so sorry. I was crying. I didn't notice or I would have asked the nurse to open the curtains because there's no reason you couldn't see Cathy Anne being baptized. I really wanted you to be able to see her baptism." I then explain what the priest did.

"That's what happened when you and Johnny were baptized when you were one month old."

Even though the outcome was not what we expected, the children could still be involved in Cathy Anne's life. I feel this nurse needs to be educated on how to help siblings in such a situation. She hasn't learned to consider the needs of her patient's family. The priest wasn't aware of the curtains being closed as far as I know.

"My grandmother made my father's baptismal gown that I and you and Johnny wore. Cathy Anne didn't have a traditional baptism with all the ceremony and party that followed. We could have a party to celebrate Cathy Anne's Baptism. I'll buy some cupcakes," I say.

"Can I have more than one?" asks Johnny.

"Sure," I say.

For several months after, Mary Christina asked, "Why did I have to miss Cathy Anne being baptized? Why did the nurse pull the curtains so I couldn't see?" I explained it, in the same way, every time she asked.

I wonder if Cathy Anne has a chance to survive or is this a hopeless situation? Our children had been looking forward to having a new baby. All their plans, hopes, and expectations must change as did ours. We explain to them that she is very sick and has to go to another hospital where she can get more care.

Before they leave, I say a prayer, "Dear God, please take care of Cathy Anne. We place her in your hands. Help us, too. Thank you, God."

When the children are leaving, Johnny puts his arms around me and says, "I miss you very much, Mommy." He looks as though he is about to cry.

I put my arms around him, kiss him, and tell him, "I miss you too. I'll be home tomorrow."

As Mary Christina is leaving, she gives me a big hug and a kiss without saying anything and walks away slowly, turning around to look at me. Her blue dress matches her big blue eyes. She raises her hand ever so slightly to wave.

CHAPTER 4

Fourteen hours after her birth, we are going
to another hospital with a NICU

Two doctors arrive and go into the newborn nursery to examine and prepare Cathy Anne for the transfer. John will be here shortly. I am standing outside the room so I can't see what they are doing. One doctor comes over to introduce himself. He has dark, wavy hair, brown eyes and is movie-star handsome.

"We'll place monitors on her so we can see how she's doing on the ride downtown. Tests will be ordered so we can find out what's causing her difficulties. Are you going to the hospital?"

"Oh yes! Can we go in the ambulance with her?"

"No, that's not allowed." He goes back into the nursery.

What else won't be allowed? How can I not be with my baby? I'm scared of what may happen. Will she die in the ambulance? What decisions will I have to make? If I have something important to say, will they shut me out or will they listen? I hope they consider our input—after all, she is our baby. I can't imagine what I can do for her, except breastfeed. Will they let me do that or do they think that formula is better? How long will I have to wait to see her?

We see Cathy Anne briefly as she is being wheeled out of the unit. She is hooked up to tubes, her color is still ashen gray. A knife may as well have stabbed my heart and broke it in half.

"I don't think she looks so bad," John says. "I'll bet the docs can fix her."

How does he not see what I see? This is not a normal looking baby. How can she survive with that color and difficulty breathing? She has some kind of syndrome, but I don't know what. Please God, help her.

Fourteen hours after her birth, we are going to another hospital that has more expertise for her diagnosis and care. No nurse or doctor says anything to me as I get ready to go. John pushes me in a wheelchair. I'm relieved the professionals didn't want me to stay. I need to follow my baby. I leave the hospital of her birth in my nightgown and robe. I don't bother with makeup. I run my fingers through my short curly hair so I won't look as disheveled as I'm feeling on the inside.

Our friend, Patti, drives us to the hospital. She has brought a present for Cathy Anne, a little blue elephant that plays, "You Are My Sunshine." The song's last line is, "Please don't take my sunshine away."

"Exactly," I say to myself.

When we arrive at the hospital I walk slowly because of the episiotomy. John gets a wheelchair so he can push me down the long halls to the Neonatal Intensive Care Unit (NICU). He wants to get to see Cathy Anne fast. There are offices to the left and right and the cream-colored walls are adorned with artwork. Paintings are for cheering people up, but nothing could do that for me. All I can think about is what is ahead for her. Will she have a treatable condition, or will she have a life-threatening illness? I realize I didn't eat anything today and I'm not hungry. My stomach is doing flip-flops.

We get to the elevator that will take us to her. It feels like forever to the 12th floor. When we arrive, it is so quiet. I wonder where the parents and staff are. We go to the nurse's station and are told to wait in the outer room until the doctors finish examining Cathy Anne. Sitting there feels like an eternity. I have never felt so helpless. We are in the dark as to what is going to happen to our baby. All we can do is hope and pray. I feel like I'm in a big black hole that I can't climb out of—I am trapped. My thoughts turn to the Blessed Mother Mary, whom I was named after, and after whom we also named our middle daughter, Mary Christina, and with whom I feel a special connection.

"Blessed Mother Mary, I beg you to help Cathy Anne and John and me cope with whatever happens to Cathy Anne. Let us be good parents to her. You are the perfect mother. Help me to be like you. Please intercede to your son, Jesus Christ, to grant our wish of a healthy Cathy Anne. Uniting my suffering with Christ's suffering on the cross is shared suffering making it bearable for me that Christ is walking with me. I offer up my emotional pain—please make Cathy Anne healthy. I know God loves me and will carry me through this ordeal. All suffering has meaning. Why was Cathy Anne born? I know her life has some purpose. I need your help in finding it. Thanks for listening."

After this prayer, my anxiety lifts. I am thankful for a faith that has taught me to have complete trust in God.

I want to talk to another parent who has a baby on this unit. One woman walks by briskly and goes inside as if she is on a mission. Perhaps she is a doctor. I want to stop her, but something inside me prevents me. I want a parent's perspective of this unit, and the care they are experiencing.

Finally, the doctor who transferred Cathy Anne here comes out with forms to sign. I am glad to see him because I feel I know him even though we had a short encounter. The doctor recommends she have an echo EKG and a cardiac catheterization. The latter unnerves me.

"A friend died having this test," I say, lips quivering. "It could happen to Cathy Anne." I'm so helpless in advocating for her. "What if she dies during the procedure?"

"I can't treat her unless I know what's going on," he responds. "The catheterization will give us the necessary information to let us see what problem her heart has. It's a risk/benefit situation and the benefits far outweigh the risks." The doctor looks at me and then at John. I can see the vein rising on John's forehead, his eyes filling with tears.

"I feel it's necessary," John tells me.

This is out of my control. I didn't want to have the ultrasound when I was pregnant and I refused it. I didn't want to expose my baby in utero to unnecessary tests. I plead with the Blessed Mother to help me with this decision.

Then I remember.

"I really don't know any of the circumstances of my friend's death several years ago," I concede. "Maybe I'm over-reacting to my friend's situation and comparing her to Cathy Anne's." I pause a moment. Benefit outweighs risks. I can give permission. "I guess you're right, John, but it's frightening."

"I see what you're saying," John presses, "but it needs to be done."

"Yes, John, you sign the papers," I say. A peace comes over me.

John looks like he is in control of the situation by the way he picks up the pen and writes his signature.

"I want to breastfeed her," I add.

"That's fine—babies are breastfed here," the doctor says.

We wait a long time to see her. I pray.

"Did you hear the cheering from the All-Star Game at Yankee Stadium?" asks John.

"No. Nothing is important except what will happen to Cathy Anne."

"For me, it was a break from the tension," says John.

This is just the beginning of our journey with Cathy Anne. John and I pray quietly together, asking God to give us strength.

CHAPTER 5

I get much comfort from John's ability to open his heart to her

After the doctors finish their preliminary examination, a process that takes a few hours, we are allowed to see her. We have to put on a green gown that will keep her from getting our germs. There is an oxygen tube in her nose, an IV in her head, and a heart monitor on her chest. She is wearing a diaper. I have no desire to touch her. She looks like she could break, which I know is impossible but that is what I think. She looks fragile like a porcelain doll. Being a nurse does not help me but makes me feel worse that I can be so detached. In fact, I think she looks ugly. What is particularly bothersome is her ashen color that signifies something is wrong and I have no idea what it is. This unknowing is like a bomb attached to my heart, ready to explode any moment and there is nothing I can do to prevent it. I do have complete trust that God will take care of Cathy Anne and me and our family.

I don't know if her condition is curable or terminal. As parents, we lack any control here. My training in nursing taught me to identify exactly what is going on. Seeing her so sick makes it difficult to bond. I don't know if she will live, die a quick death, or live a limited, marginal life. I want a diagnosis and probable outcome as quickly as possible. One moment I picture her healthy, the next minute I see our family at her grave. Over and over, I give her to

God and ask Him to hold her in the palm of His hands. I recall a Mark Twain quote, "I have been through some terrible things in my life, some of which never happened." How I wish all my anxieties were about nothing serious! I keep hoping her test results will reveal a manageable condition.

My pregnancy in contrast was uneventful. Cathy Anne had been an active baby. I was energetic, able to run after the children, swim, and play with them. I had no nausea. The troublesome pain in my legs was alleviated by heavy Jobst support stockings—such a blessing because they enabled me to do everything I had to do.

My pregnancy went on and on, well over forty weeks. The obstetrician, a partner of my usual doctor, asked for an ultrasound. "Just in case you go into labor in the middle of the night," he explained, "I wouldn't want to have to wake up the technician to come and do one."

It's the technician's job to work even in the middle of the night. All I could think is get me out of here. I jumped off the table and dressed quickly. I wasn't happy with his rationale. Ultrasounds were new at the time and I wanted to protect my child from any unnecessary tests.

How ironic that, once born, Cathy Anne needs these tests, and I can't protect her from them.

"She looks awful with all those tubes. It's hard to believe she belongs to us," I tell John.

"I don't think she looks so bad. She's just a little baby," he says.

How can he be seeing her so different from me? Is he trying to make me feel better? This doesn't help. In fact, it makes me feel worse that no one is validating how serious her condition could be.

John is able to bond with Cathy Anne and listen to me.

I get much comfort from John's ability to open his heart to her and me. He sees past her abnormality; I am grateful he can do this since I can't. What I can do is give Cathy Anne breast milk as I have done for my other two children. I feel breastfeeding is what's best. I breastfed my other two children and it was so easy, hassle-free. But Cathy Anne can't suck so this is going to be a challenge. I get very little milk when I manually express.

We leave the unit for the day. It's only twenty hours since she was born. Physically I feel fine, except for some discomfort from the episiotomy which slows down my walking. John gets a wheelchair in the hospital lobby again for me. Physically, I'm fine. I'm still wide-awake. I guess it's from my adrenaline and anxiety. Emotionally, I feel distraught over the fear of what will happen to our baby. I have a broken heart.

When we arrive home, the children are asleep which is good so we can go over with my mother what has happened. We summarize the day's happenings and then pray over them.

Prayer helps me let go of anxiety and fear as I struggle to give my daughter to God. While I know God will help her and our family, I still feel challenged living day by day. Easy to say, "Give her to God," but hard to do.

Having two beautiful, healthy children does not take away the excruciating pain of perhaps losing this child. We talk to Johnny and Mary Christina, trying to help them understand about their new sister.

Johnny asks, "Is Cathy Anne better?"

"Cathy Anne is a very sick baby," I say. "The doctors have ordered tests to see how her body is working. Let's say a prayer for Cathy Anne. Dear God, please take care of Cathy Anne and let her get better so we can enjoy her. Thank you, God, for all you have given us and bless Johnny, Mary Christina, Mommy, and Daddy and Nanny. Thank you, God."

Johnny asks, "Is she gonna get better?"

"I don't know," I answer. "The tests will tell us what her problem is. We have to wait."

Mary Christina looks at Johnny and snuggles up to me without saying anything. We are not the only ones dealing with the unknown of Cathy Anne, so must our children. I cannot take away their anxiety, but I can be there to answer their questions. Trying to help them helps me.

Later that day we go back to the hospital.

While visiting Cathy Anne is not joyful, the hospital staff is extraordinarily supportive and helpful. John manages to stroke her arms. I wonder what purpose does Cathy Anne have? Why was she born? Why go through a pregnancy, labor, and delivery if there isn't some purpose to her suffering and ours? These thoughts keep going through my mind. I would write this down over and over hoping the answer would pop out.

I know in life it's not so much as what happens to you, but what you do with what happens to you. I don't know what I will do but I know God will help me. Life is full of surprises. This was not a happy one.

At night when I can't sleep, I call the unit nurse who gives me details of how Cathy Anne is doing.

"She tolerated her feeding well," the nurse says. It is comforting to know I can call anytime and talk to the nurse caring for her. Even so, my feelings are up and down. My stomach feels like I have left it on the top of a roller coaster as it comes slamming down the rail.

I have a hand pump, but this is useless giving only about 1/8th of an ounce of milk each time. Later that night I call Barbara from La Leche League, a national organization for breastfeeding mothers, and she suggests the Gumco machine which she has on hand. John will pick it up from her.

The Gumco machine is efficient. It is the Cadillac of breast pumps. It is so important to give Cathy Anne breast milk to sustain her. Right now, she is getting colostrum, the first milk with all the immunities from me. By day three postpartum, I will have milk.

In the morning, I see my neighbors staring at me. Ralph looks at me and then down at the ground. When our eyes meet, he has a blank look. He is fidgeting with change in his pockets and shuffling his feet. He usually has something to talk about with me. Another neighbor, Carol, off to the side, has tears in her eyes. I feel like I have the plague or some awful disease. I realize they don't know what to say. I go over to them. It is almost like watching a movie, seeing what people will do. I feel detached. I smile and speak about Cathy Anne. Our neighbor Roberta has a frozen expression and says she doesn't know what to say. She doesn't want to make me cry. I assure her the feelings are there and she wouldn't be the one making me sad. Carol has tears running down her face. I go over, give her a tissue, and put my arms around her. Between tears, she says she feels so bad for our family. I thank her for her caring and say that I will let them know what happens. I ask them for their prayers and return to the house.

CHAPTER 6

"No one has ever taken a dying baby home from this hospital"

Five days after Cathy Anne's transfer to the City hospital the test results are ready. I feel hopeful that we will get good news. I call the children and we go into the living room which has windows on either side of the fireplace and two windows behind the couch where Johnny sits on John's lap and Mary Christina sits on my lap. The fireplace, the focal point of the room, has a watercolor portrait of our children above it.

"Daddy and I are going to the hospital to see what the test tells us. Let's say a prayer for Cathy Anne. Dear God, bless Cathy Anne today as we get news of her tests. Please God let there be good news for our baby. Help us to accept whatever the results will be and give us strength."

Mary Christina says, "She'll get better. I prayed to God so she'll get better."

I respond, "God hears our prayers, but we don't always get what we prayed for. We can't control what God does, we can only ask."

This hits me –how can I help this little child with her faith in God if Cathy Anne doesn't get better? I'm so helpless in trying to provide what we all want, but God isn't at our disposal to do what we want. He's not our puppet, with us pulling His strings to get our wish. It's not in our hands. So much in life is out of our control and how do we surrender to what God has in store for us? This is where faith comes in –that God will help us with whatever the outcome. How do we help our children see God's plan if it's different from ours? This is an important lesson we're all learning from Cathy Anne. We have to accept what life is dealing us. Trusting in God and turning our life over to God's will is what I have to do. This is huge. I have to respect God's plan even if I don't like it. God will give me the strength and courage to do what I need to do for Cathy Anne.

I cannot help but think of all the people who do not want their children and abuse them. We wanted our baby and looked forward to her birth. How unfair life is!

I am trying to be hopeful on the ride down to the hospital, which is a good feeling for the time being. The sun is shining, and I feel this is a sign that our life too will be sunny. However, my feelings change. One moment I have hope, the next moment I am worried she might die. I keep this to myself since John is so positive. When we arrive at the hospital, we walk the long corridors to get to the NICU. There is a lot of activity. Doctors in their white coats are walking briskly past us. RN's are walking more slowly and chatting with each other. We arrive at the elevators that will take us up to our baby. I can feel my heart beating faster and faster. I must stop for a moment and take a deep breath and let it out slowly. That helps me. Staff gets on the elevator at the next floor.

One of the doctors mentions, "Baby Wasacz." I am amazed that he pronounces *Wasacz* correctly and that is all I can focus on because many people murder my name. "WA" and "Sack" like a sack of potatoes is how I remembered to pronounce John's last name when I initially met him. Now that sounds silly, but it is a distraction to the very heavy feelings I have. When the doctor gets off the elevator, I follow him and question him about "Baby Wasacz" telling him we are the baby's parents. He does not have too much to say, only that she is "holding her own." I tell him we are going to meet with her doctor now and we part. I bet he will never mention a patient's name in a public place again. One never knows who you might be standing next to.

We meet with her doctor, who introduces us to the cardiac surgeon. I sit on the black armchair at the far corner. John sits next to me. The room is small, no windows, and white walls with a large picture of children playing in the sand at the beach. How I wish we were at the beach with our three healthy children having fun. The doctor's chair is behind a huge brown desk where he looks stern, no smile as he greets us, and shakes our hands. There is a box of tissues on top of the desk. I wonder if it is there for me in case I get bad news and cry. John sits upright with folded arms like he is protecting himself from bad news. He taps his foot up and down from time to time. He looks as though he doesn't know what to do. We are waiting with bated breath to finally find out our baby's fate.

The cardiologist states, "Cathy Anne has a heart problem and other abnormalities, all attributed to Trisomy 18, a syndrome where the extra chromosome is at the 18th position, which will cause cardiac malfunctions and severe mental retardation. The chambers of her heart are all open, which means the blood isn't circulating properly throughout her body. Besides her heart problem she could possibly have other medical complexities."

I think my heart will burst. This is far more complicated and severe than I imagined.

The doctor continues, "Further, her chance of living beyond the age of one year is slim. Ninety percent die the first month. This is a fluke of nature and you aren't carriers. This is not a hereditary condition. I don't recommend surgery on her heart because of the Trisomy and the surgery is risky which she probably wouldn't survive."

"I can't make a decision about surgery. I need time to think. Is it ethically right to withhold treatment? How can I watch her die and do nothing?" asks John.

"Let's speak with the Monsignor after Mass tomorrow," I say. As a scientist, John is analytical and needs to collect information and examine it to make a good decision. I know not to rush him.

In contrast, I'm comfortable making decisions when an explanation makes sense. I don't need more information about surgery. My nursing experience has taught me surgery is not an option. It would be prolonging the dying. Surgery will be taking extraordinary means and causing her pain. I feel it would be cruel to subject her to it. In my heart, I already know the right decision is to take her home to die.

What a mess! But I'm relieved we're not carriers. John is trying to digest all this information that he doesn't want to hear. This diagnosis also validates my feelings that there was something terribly wrong with her from the moment she was born. I am feeling like an outsider observing someone else getting this bad news.

We prayed for a good outcome, but it didn't happen. Our dreams for Cathy Anne are shattered, along with our hopes for her. We will not take her to nursery school, or ballet, or swimming lessons. She will not go to school dances or the senior prom. John will not walk her down the aisle on her wedding day. What will our Christmas be like if she dies shortly? Our plans for all the normal infant activities with her are gone. We will make her comfortable and soothe her. Hope had to change from thinking of her as a normal baby to hope that she can have some normal pleasures babies experience and that we can provide comfort for her.

"I'd like to take her home to die." *This will give me a chance to be a mother to her, even if only for a short time.*

The surgeon says, "I wouldn't do that to my children. My mother died when I was eight. I didn't go to the wake or funeral and I'm fine. No one has ever taken a dying baby home from this hospital."

"This is important to me and I don't care what other parents have done." This is a lot to digest. This surgeon is insensitive and uncaring. He does not listen to my needs. However, I am glad he shared his personal experience with us because now I can understand where he is coming from. He was not given the opportunity to be involved in the death of his mother. If he didn't share this with us, I would have been angry with him telling me what I should do with my baby. I feel my children will be able to handle having their little sister home. Death is a part of life and when the situation arises it is important to have them involved in their own way.

The cardiologist says, "Be glad you have two healthy children. One mother here has no children and is watching her third baby dying of a heart condition."

I'm not interested in anyone else's heartache. I'm only absorbed in my own sorrow.

"What are my chances of this happening again?" I ask.

"Since this abnormality happened once, the chances increase that it could happen again. Would you have an abortion if it occurred?"

"No, I wouldn't have an abortion."

"Since you wouldn't have an abortion, I would advise you not to have any more children."

Now, I'm dealing with the impending loss of Cathy Anne and all future children. How devastating! I wanted a large family. I'm an only child so I always thought I'd like ten children. My two children are a joy and I love being a mother to them which reinforces my having more children.

"Unfortunately, the Trisomy 18 could happen again," says the surgeon, as he gets up from his chair and leaves the room so John and I can talk.

CHAPTER 7

By listening and talking about our concerns we can help each other

"I can't take her home," says John as he fidgets in his chair. He clears his throat several times, tapping his feet up and down and stares into my eyes. "You do everything right; eat well, help people. What a tragedy." He grabs my hand. His palms are cold and sweaty.

"We can't abandon her. We'll manage," I reply.

How can he not want to take her home? This is not the John I know. What has happened to him? How can John be so afraid of this tiny baby? John is an accomplished professional and can always tackle any problem. He is probably overwhelmed facing the diagnosis he never expected to get.

"Remember the Marriage Encounter a few months ago? We agreed we'd take care of our parents?"

"That's different—not our baby."

John looks at me as though I am speaking a foreign language while he is staring blankly into space. How can I reach him?

"Why don't you want to take her home?" He is sweating, looking down at his feet when he finally replies, staring right in my eyes.

"I'm afraid of being alone if she dies. You know how you say you'll be back in an hour, but come sauntering in several hours later from shopping?"

"I'm sorry. I do have the habit of saying I will shop for an hour but wind-up shopping for much longer," I apologize. I get so caught up looking in different stores for clothes, gadgets, and items for the children. Shopping is pure joy! Especially when Johnny and Mary Christina are not in tow. I completely forget about the time.

I reassure John, "I won't leave you alone with Cathy Anne. I know it would be terrifying for you if she died and you were home alone with her."

"I can't think. I can't imagine taking her home," says John.

This touches me. I have to respect his concerns, but I don't like it. His face is white, his shoulders slouched. He unfolds his arms and grabs my hand. I am glad for the strength in his hand which I need. This is a blow to what I think I can do for Cathy Anne. Since John is adamant, I don't see further conversation helping either one of us. He is stuck in his thinking and does not want to get unstuck. I want our baby to have whatever is possible for me, John, and our children to do for her. I am willing to pump breast milk, visit her in the hospital, and learn the skills I need. How am I going to live with his decision? What is to become of Cathy Anne and my role as a mother? He has a dazed look.

"How will we cope? What will Johnny and Mary Christina think?" asks John as he sits upright in his chair as though glued to the seat. "I can't take her home," he finally says.

If we don't take her home, she will be transferred to an institution to be cared for. The hospital won't keep her, once they know there is no treatment for her.

We both had different experiences growing up and learning about death and we brought those experiences to this moment with our daughter. My mother took care of her mother, my grandmother, when she got sick. She was sick for about six months. On her last day, my parents and I were sitting in the dining room having lunch when suddenly we heard a door slam. We ran inside my grandmother's room. She had died. The door was open, and no other door had slammed. We prayed over her. The explanation my mother came up with was that my grandmother went to heaven and the door to earth was slammed shut. This positive experience made a lasting impression on me. From this experience, I thought everyone should die at home surrounded by loved ones. Our house was filled with love. I had a sister born before me who lived eight hours. I always knew about her and it wasn't scary for me. She was still a part of our family even though she lived in heaven.

John's family handled death differently. He did not go to his grandfather's funeral but doesn't know why. He was five years old. He didn't attend his grandmother's funeral but thinks there was not enough room in the car traveling to Pennsylvania from New York. He was eleven years old. When he was about twelve years old, he was teased by a cousin that he was not the firstborn. He learned he had a brother who was stillborn. He was shocked and angry at the cousin. He didn't want to upset his parents since they never mentioned it to him, so he never brought it up. Death became a mysterious, forbidden topic. However, the first time his dad talked about his baby that died was when I had a miscarriage. His dad was very supportive of John and he was to his father.

By listening and talking about our concerns we can help each other. I need patience with John until he can process this information. I must respect his feelings.

CHAPTER 8

Cathy Anne has a right to be home with us

John and I take time away from the hospital with good friends Barbara and Joe. Joe is a colleague of John's. They have two small children that play with Mary Christina and Johnny at college functions and for regular playdates.

"We're going to Beef and Ale in Riverdale for dinner," says Joe.

"That sounds great to me," says John. "I haven't had much of an appetite the last few days. I could really use a good meal now."

As we are driving up the Henry Hudson Parkway, we can see the Palisades across the river. The George Washington Bridge looks majestic with the backdrop of the vibrant green foliage on the cliff-side. The Hudson River is calm today. I find water scenes soothing. The huge apartment buildings remind me of the days we lived in an apartment when we were first married. John came home for lunch every day which we enjoyed. These are beautiful memories! Finally, we arrive at the restaurant.

This is our first time in this restaurant. It's rustic with scenic pictures on the walls of farms and animals. There are pink carnations on the table with a white lit candle next to it. The lights are dim and this adds to the ambiance of the room.

"How was your meeting?" asks my friend Barbara.

"We found out from the cardiac surgeon that Cathy Anne has Trisomy 18," I explain. "We were advised not to have any more children since I wouldn't have an abortion. It's hard enough losing one child but now our hope for a large family is gone."

"Mary, I'm so sorry. That's such terrible news," says Barbara as she stares into my eyes. She looks like she is about to cry.

Joe turns to us, saying, "My heart goes out to you. If I can do anything …"

"Pray for Cathy Anne and our family," I tell him.

"We have been praying," says Joe.

"You're not just a colleague but a good friend," remarks John.

"I can't believe it," I say.

"Nor can I. What a shock," says John.

Here we are, five days after her birth, which we were anticipating with such joy, only to have it shattered with the dreaded news of her condition. If I have the chance to be a mother to her, even for a short time, it will make the pregnancy worthwhile.

"We're happy to be here with you and Joe. This is a welcome relief from all the decisions we have to make at the hospital. I knew something was terribly wrong when Cathy Anne was born but hoped it wouldn't be fatal," I say.

"I'm sorry Cathy Anne got such a terrible diagnosis. We thought you were having a healthy baby," says Barbara.

I respond, "Right now, I have to focus on Cathy Anne for however long we have her."

I'm relaxed for the first time since she was born. It is almost magical, transporting me to another place where I feel like I don't have a care in the world. I will relish this moment. I will enjoy my dinner of surf and turf, savoring every bite. We make small talk about our children who often play with Meghan and Mary Beth, Barbara and Joe's children. When dinner is over, they drive us home.

After our arrival, John walks around the kitchen looking preoccupied. I wonder what he's thinking. Later that night he tells me,

"You know, Cathy Anne has as much a right to be home with us as Johnny and Mary Christina. It's her house too. She should be at home. But I'm still thinking about coping with her dying here."

"I'd be thrilled to have her home. Take your time, no rush."

"What made you change your mind?"

"Being in the kitchen, looking at all the work my dad and I are doing, it hit me, Cathy Anne is our baby and needs to be home with us."

Wow, he certainly is coming around despite his fears. I'm so lucky to have him for a husband. He always listens to me when I'm upset. I appreciate him so much. He has always been my best friend and confidant. My prayers to St. Anthony for a good husband have paid off. I never thought we'd face a dying child. I'll keep praying.

Early in the morning, the children come running into our bedroom and want to hear all about Cathy Anne. We go downstairs into the living room.

I sit on the rust and white-flowered couch. Mary Christina climbs onto my lap. John sits on the rust-striped upholstered rocking chair. Johnny climbs onto his lap.

Mary Christina is quiet and just looks at Johnny and then at me.

"Is Cathy Anne better?" asks Johnny.

"No. Cathy Anne is very sick. She has an illness that only a newborn baby can get. The message inside Cathy Anne is all mixed up and wrong," says John.

"You mean we have pencil and paper inside making notes?" asks Johnny.

"Something like that," says John.

I didn't want them to worry that they or we could get her disease and die.

"We have to make Cathy Anne comfortable and love her. She will probably only live a short time," I say.

"Oh," says Johnny. "Can we have breakfast now? I'm hungry."

Mary Christina just looks at me with her big blue eyes. Both children jump off our laps and run into the kitchen.

John and I look at each other. John says, "Well, so much for a deep conversation with a three and five-year-old." We both chuckle.

"Yeah, that's normal. They have to process a little at a time."

As a psychiatric nurse, I am acquainted with the power of emotions and grief, and their need for space and time. They have a short attention span, so we have to follow their lead. That's what attracted me to the field where I need to be tender towards people in pain.

CHAPTER 9

She probably wouldn't survive the surgery

"I have many things to process. It's happening so fast. Surgery, no surgery. Am I failing as her father? I'm supposed to protect her. I have to speak for Cathy Anne." John winces and looks at me. His brow is furrowed. "I took moral theology in college. Putting her through surgery would be taking extraordinary means. How can I live with myself if I deny her surgery?"

I can see the pain on John's face as he grapples with the surgery question. His head is down, tears are in his eyes. His face is pale. I put my arms around him and kiss him.

"From my nursing experience, surgery's out. It's equivalent to CPR on someone dying from stage four cancer, the last stage of cancer."

"Let's talk with Monsignor," says John.

The next day we see Monsignor after Mass in the parking lot. His face is moist in the early morning light. We stand near the grotto of the Blessed Mother, a serene and isolate location on the side of the church. It has a calming effect on me. A gentle breeze crosses my face.

John explains to the Monsignor about Cathy Anne's condition. He asks the Monsignor,

"Is it ethically okay not to do the surgery?"

"Yes, it is. Surgery isn't necessary because of the gravity of her condition. It would be putting her through undo suffering. She probably wouldn't survive the surgery."

"That's what the doctor said," replies John.

"You can continue to love her and care for her. That's being active and doing something essential for her."

"So, I can focus on what I can do for her. We'll be taking her home where it's easier to love her," says John.

"Thanks, Monsignor. You've been a big help to both of us," I say.

As we're walking toward the car, I ask, "How are you, John?"

"I feel like a huge boulder has been lifted from my shoulders. I can live with my decision. No surgery."

CHAPTER 10

It's heartbreaking to see how they are looking forward to meeting their sister who will be here for only a short time

The children are in the den on the floor drawing pictures for Cathy Anne. The den is John's office with a brown leather couch, a rosewood desk, and a chair. Two windows face the front of the house with the rosewood desk underneath. Rosewood bookcases line the wall opposite three windows along the side of the house. I walk into the room saying, "Tomorrow we'll bring you to the hospital to see Cathy Anne."

"I can't wait to play with her," says Johnny. He jumps up and down waving his picture in the air. Mary Christina joins in the jumping, waving her picture in the air, singing,

"Yeah, yeah we're gonna see Cathy Anne."

"Remember how you practiced holding your dolls and stuffed animals?" I remind them.

"Oh yeah. We have to be careful with her head," Johnny motions with his hands.

"I'll be careful with her head," says Mary Christina.

"I don't think you'll get to hold her tomorrow because she has a tube in her nose that gives her oxygen so she can breathe easier. There's a tube in her head giving her water, so she won't be thirsty. A monitor listens to her heart so the nurses know she's okay."

I want to prepare them for what they will see so they will not be frightened.

The next morning the children wake up early so they can get ready for their visit with Cathy Anne. Mary Christina and Johnny come running down the stairs for breakfast, the two of them elbowing each other to be the first down.

"You look beautiful. And you look handsome," I say.

"Look, my favorite pink dress. I'm gonna give Cathy Anne my little cookie monster and the picture I drew."

Johnny looks at his dad also wearing khaki pants and a blue and green striped shirt. He exclaims, "Yippee, yippee," jumping up and down, yelling "we're wearing the same thing! I wanna give Cathy Anne my favorite purple rabbit."

Both children are wearing their dress shoes. Mary Christina has black Mary Jane party shoes on and Johnny has his brown leather loafers.

I can see how important this visit is to them. I am surprised they wore their dressy clothes. They see it as a party and dress for the occasion along with presents for her, making this special in their mind, but not in my mind. It's heartbreaking to see how they are looking forward to meeting their sister who will be here for only a short time.

It's hard for me to make a decision about the simplest thing to do or what to wear. I finally put on a red loose-fitting dress, so I won't look so fat. My mother comes downstairs wearing a blue dress and blue high heels. She's looking forward to seeing her granddaughter.

The atmosphere in the car is a happy one, which makes me forget the grave condition of Cathy Anne. It is a break from the heavy, sad feelings that permeated my thinking since she was born. My mother reminds us of God's love for us and His help in coping with Cathy Anne. My mother always has a way of making me feel better, even if it is short-lived. We are grateful for any time we will have with Cathy Anne and see this as a blessing. Cathy Anne is named after my mother, Catherine, my grandmother, Anne, and my Aunt Anna.

"Let's say three Hail Mary's for Cathy Anne and ask God's blessing on her and all of us," I say.

My mother is in the back seat with the children and together they sing some of their favorite songs they will sing to Cathy Anne. "Jesus loves the little children, all the children of the world." When we arrive, the children get out of the car and hold Nanny's hands, happy to meet their sister.

CHAPTER 11

I pick her up for the first time since the day she was born

We walk the long hallway to the NICU. Johnny and Mary Christina notice the staff coming out of the cafeteria carrying ice cream cones.

"Can we get a cone?" asks Johnny.

"Me too?" asks Mary Christina.

"Yes, you can, after we visit with Cathy Ann," I say.

"Wow, isn't it a busy place? It must be a good hospital to take a sick baby," I say. We ride the elevator to the 12th floor and are taken to the family room so we can have privacy. The room has salmon paint on the walls and a comfortable brown leather couch with a cushioned back against the wall for our family to relax against while holding Cathy Anne.

John, Nanny and I wear green scrub gowns to protect Cathy Anne from germs. The children wear white Johnny coats over their party clothes.

"I like this white thing I'm in," says our Johnny. Mary Christina looks at her brother without saying anything.

I bring a little blue elephant, a present from a friend to give to Cathy Anne.

When the nurse wheels Cathy Anne in, she is no longer in the iso-lette, but in a bassinet wearing a pink, stretchy outfit. All the tubes have been removed.

"She looks so different without all those tubes," I say.

"She looks normal to me," says John.

"But she is a very sick baby," I remind John.

I can't believe I'm actually going to hold her. I pick her up for the first time since the day she was born. What a wonderful feeling to have her in my arms which doesn't seem real. Am I dreaming? She makes a baby noise. How sweet! She has a delicious newborn scent, skin so soft, and fits so easily into my arms, which make me feel like a mother. I'm grateful she didn't die before I had this chance. Her life is uncertain and I will cherish each moment with her. I give her to Nanny. She is thrilled to hold Cathy Anne. I don't want to give her up, but everyone needs to have their turn. She holds her briefly and then gives her to John.

John looks so comfortable with her. He is smiling. He tells her, "You're beautiful. I love you. You will come home with us so you can be part of our family in our house, your house."

"Wow, John. That means a lot." John gives me a big grin and a kiss on my cheek. I feel so happy, so complete. I will be delighted to have our little angel home with us. I will be able to care for her and be her mother. I can't imagine anyone else taking care of her. John kisses her on the forehead and gives her to Johnny.

Johnny holds her so carefully, gently touching her head on the left side, looking at her face, taking in her features. My heart is breaking in two. *Many thoughts bombard my mind. How long will we have her? How will I manage her and my two energetic children? How will I keep their life normal when there is nothing normal about our situation?*

Mary Christina is patiently waiting for her turn to hold Cathy Anne. Johnny knows he has to share her, and he is okay when I pick her up and place her in Mary Christina's arms. I hear a baby noise when she is moved. It's an adorable sound. Mary Christina stares at her, looking into her eyes, singing, "Love you, Cathy Anne." A bittersweet feeling washes over me. I will savor the image of my children together, yes, all three, enjoying this moment which I will hold in my heart forever.

MEETING CATHY ANNE FOR THE FIRST TIME

Family photos in the hospital. Johnny and Mary Christina meet Cathy Anne for the first time.

John and I wear green johnny coats, the children wear white johnny coats to protect Cathy Anne from germs.

We all take turns holding Cathy Anne. Johnny and Mary Christina are very careful holding her. Cathy Anne's tubes have been removed. She is dressed in a cute pink and white onesie.

*My mother, Catherine "Kitty" Perry on the
upper left and John's mother, Mary Wasacz,
holds Cathy Anne as Johnny looks at her.*

CHAPTER 12

I feel people should die at home with family

John informs the nurse that we want to bring Cathy Anne home to die. The nurse arranges for the doctor to meet with us the following morning. The next day we meet with him.

He says, "I think it's great you want to take her home. No one has ever requested this before. Half the staff will think it's great, the other half will think you're nuts."

"I don't care what anyone thinks. It's important to me."

"I served in Vietnam. The culture there is very different from here. Parents took care of their dying babies at home. I spoke with your pediatrician and he's going to be the primary doctor for Cathy Anne. I'll be back up," informs the doctor.

"My grandmother died at home when I was twelve. I feel people should die at home with their family," I respond.

"It seems like that was a positive experience for you."

"I'd like to take her to a picnic with John's colleagues."

"That's fine but realize she could die at any time, even at the picnic."

"I will try to go on with my life as best I can."

"That's a good way to be. There are a few things we will teach you about caring for Cathy Anne. I would like the nurse to observe you pass the gastric tube a few times before you take her home," the doctor says.

"I agree. I'm a psych nurse and could use a refresher on how to pass the tube."

The doctor suggests, "Keep a journal and enter in it each day. Record your feelings, how you're doing and how well Cathy Anne is responding to your care. Other thoughts might be how your other children cope with their dying sister."

Later that day the nurse shows me how to pass the gastric tube. The gastric tube is placed in through Cathy Anne's nose and down into her stomach. I have to pull back on a syringe to ensure that the fluid is in her stomach and not in her lungs. This could cause her to aspirate. I do this easily two times. I feel confident bringing her home.

CHAPTER 13

For a moment it feels like Cathy Anne is a normal baby

Finally, seven days after her birth, we are taking her home. This has been the longest week of my life. I don't know if she will live a while or die quickly and what will I do? What will my family do? I realize I must take one day at a time and not worry about tomorrow. I must focus on the moments we have with her.

The sun is shining. We are thrilled today, wild with anticipation. The children and Nanny stay home to wait for John's mother, his two sisters, their husbands, and three cousins to come and spend the day with us to celebrate Cathy Anne's life. John's dad picks us up and drives us to the hospital. I am glad my father-in-law, whom we and the children call Dad, is with us for Cathy Anne's trip home.

"There isn't any traffic. I hope it's the same coming home," says Dad.

"That's a good sign. I can't wait to hold Cathy Anne," I say.

"I'm happy she's coming home. Thanks for being patient," says John.

"I know you and I know when I have to back off. Are you happy you changed your mind?"

"Yes," John agrees.

Finally, we arrive at the hospital, walk the long hall to the elevator where we get on to go up to the 12th floor. The children helped me pack pink socks, a pink sundress, diapers, and a Winnie-the-Pooh receiving blanket for Cathy Anne. When we arrive on the unit, we go to the nurse's station and are told to go into the conference room. I am beside myself with anticipation waiting for her to come to us.

"I can't believe she's actually coming home today."

"Nor can I," says John.

Dad is a comfort, supporting us with his presence. The nurse comes in with Cathy Anne in a bassinet. I will feed her one more time before taking her home. The tube goes into her nose and down her stomach with ease. I pull back on the syringe to make sure the tube is not in her lungs. I pour the breast milk into the syringe and it passes slowly. John holds her while I do this.

We say goodbye and thank the nurses for all their help, and we are on our way. I am holding Cathy Anne in my arms, I feel like I am walking on air. I glide as I leave the unit and get on the elevator and walk the long halls. God is with us. This is not the homecoming of our new baby we had anticipated. How I wish she had been healthy.

What a beautiful ride home! Cathy Anne sleeps. I can enjoy the scenery going up the West Side Highway, looking at the river and the Palisades. The high-rise buildings overlooking the river are breathtaking. Dad talks about going to the City and the fun he and Grandma had dating. His sister, Kay, introduced them. *I feel content and peaceful. I wish this moment could last forever. I know it is temporary because she can die any time. I hope we will be prepared and have some warning. Who knows what we will experience? I know God will be with us and for this I am grateful.*

We finally arrive home. I am filled with excitement to watch our family meet Cathy Anne. When John opens the door, I can smell the delicious roast my mother has prepared along with the stuffed cabbage John's mother has made. The cabbage, a traditional Polish dish; the roast, an Irish/American dish. We enjoy combining the different cultures in our family and all benefit from it. These are two of our favorite dinners and it is great having them today to celebrate Cathy Anne's homecoming. All gather around me as I sit on the couch holding her. The children are bubbling with excitement, jumping up and down, and laughing. For a moment it feels like Cathy Anne is a normal baby, but that feeling lasts a few seconds when I come back to reality—she is a very sick newborn with a limited life expectancy.

Lunch is ready. The table is set in the living room since the dining room is occupied by my dishes from the kitchen cabinets for the remodeling of our kitchen. Flowers from our garden are on the table. There is a magnificent aroma from the gardenias that permeate the room. My mother put on a beautiful tablecloth with red grapes and green vines flowing all over. How we all enjoy this family gathering,

"Can I hold Cathy Anne when she wakes up?" says Johnny and each child asks the same question and are told they can. They are happy to have a baby to hold and to love.

Cathy Anne sleeps all through our dinner. I have a chance to relax and enjoy the food. Just as dessert of mint chocolate chip ice cream is finished, I hear her faint little cry. I go over to feed her. I have the tube, the syringe, and the breast milk all ready. My mother holds her while I pass the tube. As I pass the tube through her tiny nostril it gets stuck and comes out the way it went in. She is fighting the tube. I realize, silly me, this is a reflex. What a disaster! She has to get nourishment or she will die. Now what am I going to do? Who can I call? I think of a nurse, Chris, I had taught with at Mount Sinai School of Nursing. Recently she moved down the street from me. I pray she will be home.

"Hi Chris," I explain the situation

"I'll be right over."

This never happened in the hospital. Chris arrives and passes the tube smoothly and suggests I keep the tube in her nose using paper tape she has brought. We have a visit and she tells me I can call her anytime. Thank God for good friends. She was a maternal child nurse. I knew she would know how to pass a tube. I was a psychiatric nurse. I could talk about my feelings about a tube, but it wouldn't help in this situation.

The family sits quietly while all this is going on. I am grateful they didn't add any comments to this stressful situation. I am happy they are here and can support us as we learn how to take care of our baby. Cathy Anne has fallen asleep. The children will have to wait for her to wake up to hold her. I suggest the children be taken to the park. John's parents, his two younger sisters and my brother in-laws supervise all the children at the nearby park. Nanny, John and I stay home to collect our thoughts and recuperate from this trying situation. It is good for us to be with adults who are caring and supporting us in our decision to bring her home. We feel loved. What a homecoming she had!

CATHY ANNE'S HOMECOMING

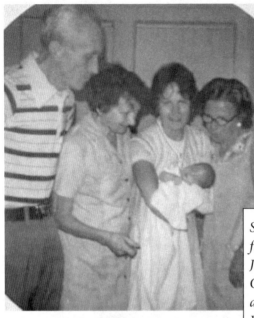

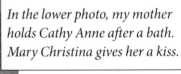

Surrounded by our parents, from the left, John's father, John Wasacz, my mother, Catherine "Kitty" Perry, and John's mother, Mary Wasacz. I hold Cathy Anne.

In the lower photo, my mother holds Cathy Anne after a bath. Mary Christina gives her a kiss.

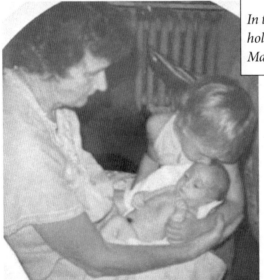

MY THREE CHILDREN

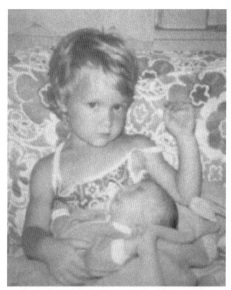

Mary Christina holds Cathy Anne on the couch at our home in Westchester County, New York.

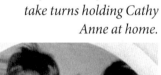

Johnny and Mary Christina take turns holding Cathy Anne at home.

YOU ARE MY SUNSHINE

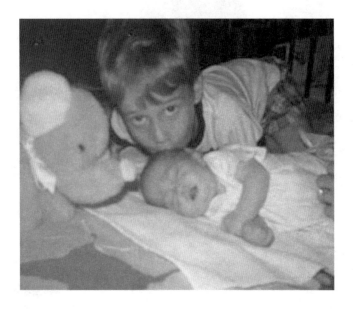

Cathy Anne is pictured above with Johnny and her little blue elephant. When wound, the elephant's head swayed and carried the tune, "You Are My Sunshine." This beautiful lullaby by Jimmie Davis came to have special meaning associated with Cathy Anne's life and death.

Even today, hearing the last line, "please don't take my sunshine away" reminds me of the little blue elephant and my little girl.

CHAPTER 14

Always on my mind, "When will she die? Will I be prepared?"

I try to keep our children's days as routine as possible to provide some normalcy to their lives. They have their friends to play with and activities to attend. Cathy Anne, a contented baby, rarely cries except when hungry. Her cry is weak and soft. Holding her after feeding is peaceful for me. My days start at 6AM but Johnny and Mary Christina are asleep till about 7:30. This lets my mother and me give full attention to Cathy Anne. John usually leaves for work at this time.

My mother holds Cathy Anne and sings to her while I tube-feed her, a nice routine we have every day. My mother is thrilled to be able to hold her. I can still hear my mother's sweet voice singing, "Teach me how to pray! God was just your little boy, Tell me what to say! Did you lift Him up, sometimes, gently on your knee?"

When Johnny and Mary Christina wake up each day, they want to see their baby sister. They give her a kiss and run downstairs for breakfast. Nanny goes with them while I linger with Cathy Anne.

And so, the day begins. We go for strolls with Mary Christina and Johnny.

Johnny says, "I wanna push the stroller first."

"No," says Mary Christina. "I wanna push first."

"You can push her together."

As I look at my children, I wonder how I'll handle all this—my healthy, energetic children and my dying baby. My children can turn a simple activity into work for me. It's hard being patient with Johnny and Mary Christina while worrying about Cathy Anne. How am I going to get through this day? It's only 10:30 and already I'm exhausted–not from the physical care of Cathy Anne— she's no trouble. It's the emotional worry about her that makes me exhausted, while trying to be available to Johnny and Mary Christina.

After a short distance, Mary Christina tells her brother, "You push her."

Mary Christina is happy to walk beside Cathy Anne. Later, she has her turn. Both children are helping Cathy Anne enjoy her day. I wish I had time to take a nap. Always on my mind is when will she die? Will I be prepared? Will I be okay?

When we come home from our walk, it is bath time. How Cathy Anne loves her bath! A sponge bath. Her umbilical cord has not fallen off so she can't soak in water. She seems content as I wash her brown hair. I hold her in a football position using a bar of soap and a duck-shaped yellow washcloth. She looks at me right into my eyes. I wish she were healthy.

"I'll get my favorite towel," says Mary Christina, running as she goes to the linen closet, returning with a pink towel with yellow, blue and green flowers.

The radio is playing "Looks Like We Made It" by Barry Manilow.

Johnny says, "I wanna hear '(Frere Jacques) Are You Sleeping?' Cathy Anne would like it."

"OK," I say. He gets the tape and plays the lullaby. Music soothes us. The children like to do things for Cathy Anne. What a shame she will never play with them.

Lunch time for Johnny and Mary Christina is a fun time. What joy they have in spreading the peanut butter and slicing the banana. Much of the peanut butter sticks to the bread in bunches, but they wash it down with milk. Cathy Anne will never make her own peanut butter and banana sandwich.

Johnny and Mary Christina like to hold Cathy Anne. They take turns and each one is gentle and caring. When I see the three together, my heart feels like a knife has ripped my heart out of my body. She can be snatched from us at any time. The children know she is very sick and dying. Their beloved cat, Snowball, died two weeks before Cathy Anne was born. We found him dead in the street after being hit by a car. This gave us the opportunity to talk about Snowball with the children and bury him. The children participated in his funeral. God sent Snowball to prepare our children for Cathy Anne's death.

A new baby requires lots of attention. A dying newborn adds much to the situation.

I take Johnny to the pool, while Mary Christina has a birthday party to attend and Nanny is watching Cathy Anne at home. It is a beautiful, sunny day. Johnny, standing by the side of the pool, looks forlorn. I worry that he feels burdened. My first thought is that he must be depressed. I go over to him and put my arms around him. I kiss him on his forehead, and he feels hot. He has a fever. He isn't depressed. I am so relieved! What mother is happy for their child to have a fever? Situations certainly change one's thinking. He's fine when we get home. He probably didn't have a fever. He was just hot from the sun and being outside at the pool.

Life with Cathy Anne is an experience I never could have imagined. This is a nightmare I wish I could wake up from. The mental anguish permeates my very being. How can I help Johnny and Mary Christina with each issue that surfaces? Fortunately, John is a strong supporter in all I do which I appreciate. God walks with me and I know I can count on Him with whatever happens in our life. Trusting in Him always helps but the human side of me creeps in making me fearful of what I will be like when she dies.

CHAPTER 15

A friend says it would have been bet-
ter if Cathy Anne died right away

My neighbor, Chloe, the owner of a Fitness Center, gives me a gift certificate to her gym. I was always skinny and never exercised, never gained weight and never had to watch what I ate, but after my third pregnancy, I am fat. This fat abdomen is a reminder of Cathy Anne. I join the gym. This is a wonderful experience helping me with grief. I feel I am accomplishing good for my body. While exercising, I go over thoughts of Cathy Anne which lead to profound sadness. But the repetitions of exercises feel good. Had I not received this gift, I never would have joined a gym, a healing activity I continue to this day.

In addition to the fitness classes, I meet with my friend Sonja. Sonja, a special education teacher, was in a Lamaze class I taught. Sonja visits and offers suggestions to stimulate Cathy Anne. One is having Cathy Anne face a mirror making circles on the mirror with pudding on her hands. When Sonja says to put a round toy in Cathy Anne's hands, so her fingers won't be in a fixed position, Johnny offers to get his tinker toys. He runs upstairs and comes back with two red and blue round pegs that are perfect for her little hands. He is so excited he can do something for his baby sister.

Sonja tells us to have Cathy Anne follow an object left to right.

Johnny says, "I'll get Brown Teddy. I wouldn't give him to anybody but Cathy Anne." He runs upstairs to his room and brings Brown Teddy down quickly. It makes a squeaky sound when squeezed which she seems to respond to.

"Sonja, thanks for these tips. I feel I'm doing something to make her life more enjoyable which helps me in being a mother to Cathy Anne."

Our parish priest, Stuart, comes to visit. John and I will always be grateful for Stuart's wise counsel. Stuart comes by weekly to offer support and prayer to our family. While I'm not home, my mother is, and he gives her the opportunity to share her hesitation to go on her long-ago planned vacation to Florida. When I come home, my mother says, "Stuart came while you were out and blessed Cathy Anne and me. He encourages me to go to Florida."

"That's great. You should go. You can't put your life on hold indefinitely. The statistics could be in her favor. Ten percent of babies with Trisomy 18 make it to a year, of course ninety percent die within the first month. We don't know how long Cathy Anne will live. You should go."

"Maybe," replies my mother.

"You should make plans for the trip."

"I still want to think about it."

"It's your decision, but I think you could use a trip after all the help you've given us. You're doing so much work here, doing laundry, cooking, and taking care of everyone. We will be okay," I assured her.

"I need more time to think about it," my mother replied.

Over the course of the next few weeks, several other friends stop by. Some offer encouraging words and helpful advice. Others unknowingly hurt me deeply.

Julie, a nurse from Cathy Anne's hospital comes to visit. She arrives with much needed feeding tubes for Cathy Anne. Julie gave an excellent presentation on a neonatal unit when she was a nursing student of mine at Pace University. This was another reason I chose Julie's prominent New York hospital for Cathy Anne's care. I'm grateful and thankful for all the support I had in my sad journey with Cathy Anne.

We love getting visitors, but I'm amazed and disappointed at the hurtful things people can say, thinking they're being kind. A close friend visits and remarks, "It would have been better if Cathy Anne died right away." *How cruel. She is also a mother. How could she say this to me? She hasn't asked me how I feel. What a horrible thing to say.*

In disbelief, I have the courage to say, "That's not particularly helpful. I'm happy I have the chance to be her mother, if only for a short time." She seems to accept what I say.

Although I thought this was my last negative experience with my friends, Allison comes to see how I am. We spend time talking over tea and she holds Cathy Anne. She looks me straight in the eye and says, "You're young, you can have other children." *To me it's like saying, 'You broke a lamp, you can go buy a new lamp.' I know she is trying to make me feel better but it's not so simple. I wish it were.* "I want this baby, and another baby would never take away my sorrow for Cathy Anne. I might not be able to have another baby. My doctor advised me not to have more children." *I realized from this encounter with Allison that in an effort to make me feel better, she gave me an unrealistic solution that she was unaware.*

Another friend calls me. I tell her my baby has a terminal condition. She immediately hangs up. I'm learning through this situation the friends I can and cannot count on for advice, kindness and strength.

June comes to visit and says, "You can do this because you're a nurse. I never could take care of a dying child." I'm surprised again by my friends' blunt honesty. Her statement is off-base. "I don't think my being a nurse has any bearing. I'm just a mother who wants to take care of her baby. I'm happy she's here at home." *I'm learning more about myself. I am capable of dealing with an unthinkable situation. It is unnatural for a baby to die before its parents. It goes against nature. I know I made the right decision to bring Cathy Anne home. I am her best advocate and have inner strength I never thought I had. This has prepared me for anything life will bring.*

I learn I am not alone with experiencing strange interactions with friends. When John comes home from the lab, he shares his experiences doing a summer postdoc at Columbia University. He tells me of a co-worker's behavior.

"When one researcher walks by me, he puts his paper in front of his face. Several other researchers duck into an office rather than approach me. It is like watching a movie of these people avoiding me at all costs."

"It's almost funny picturing grown, educated colleagues avoiding you in such a ridiculous manner. It makes me laugh. Don't take it personally. It's not you. They don't know what to say to you. They don't want to hurt your feelings."

"I won't take this personally."

"If you want to talk with anyone, you're going to have to make the first move," I tell him.

"You're right. I probably need to break the ice about chemistry or research to let them know it's okay to talk to me."

People say the darndest things or avoid John and me altogether. Some friends in the medical profession are also at a loss as to what to say. They are too scientific in their conversations with us. A light bulb goes off. It is an aha moment. John and I will give talks to professionals on the emotional aspects of parents dealing with a dying baby. I've found Cathy Anne's purpose. This idea makes me feel good. Something positive will come out of Cathy Anne's brief life. We are invited to give talks in schools of nursing, hospitals, churches, and colleges.

CHAPTER 16

I am shocked at the words that come out of my mouth

A few days later I am standing outside. Our neighbor frantically points at my upstairs bedroom window. She says, "Mary Christina is pushing her head against the screen!"

I run upstairs taking two steps at a time so I will get to Mary Christina quickly. What if she falls out the window? What would happen to her?

"Mary Christina, come here," I say so softly. She backs away from the window. I race over to get her away from the window and hug her.

"It's very dangerous to push against the screen. It can pop out and you'll fall out the window. You can get hurt." She looks at me without saying anything. She is not aware of the dangerous situation. Mary Christina runs outside to be with her friends. I realize I could have lost Mary Christina. My healthy daughter. My heart sinks. I breed resentment towards my sick infant. These are feelings I did not have before. I was angry.

I go into our bedroom where Nanny and Cathy Anne are. All of a sudden, I look at Cathy Anne and shout out, "God damn, Cathy Anne, you really messed up my life." I am shocked at what comes out of my mouth, but it is the truth.

"Oh, you don't mean that," my mother says.

I snap back at her, "Yes I do."

Then I am angry with my mother for telling me how I should feel. But the anger passes quickly. My mother is very understanding, and my outburst wasn't a problem for her. I never swear and never take God's name in vain and can't believe what I said. Still, I feel much better having confronted my anger at Cathy Anne who messed up my life, which I was unaware of before. Will my life ever be easy again? I don't know what the future will hold for us.

CHAPTER 17

I have to sit with these uncomfortable feel-ings and continue to pray for strength

I enjoy holding Cathy Anne and smelling her newborn scent. How sad it will be for all of us when she dies. I know I am fine now when she's alive, but what will I be like when she dies? How will John and our children be? What long-term effect will she have on Johnny and Mary Christina? These are my recurrent thoughts.

The phone rings.

"Hi Mary, this is Ellen."

I am so happy to hear from Ellen. She is my closest friend and was my maid of honor. John and I go on dates and weekend vacations to the Poconos and Connecticut with Ellen and her husband Kevin. She is the sibling I never had.

"Kevin and I are wondering if you would like a prayer group to come and pray over Cathy Anne."

"Yes, that would be lovely. A prayer group would mean so much to me. Especially since prayer and love is all we can do for her now."

I know a miracle is a pretty far-fetched idea, but God can do anything and make her whole. Miracles come in different ways. Physical healing is one type of miracle; spiritual healing is another. Our prayer is for physical healing, but if this doesn't happen our prayer is that our family will be alright. I know God will be there for me; I trust in Him. Prayer and talking to God gives me comfort.

Ellen and Kevin come with several church members to offer prayer and support. It is a blur how many people came. One of the members, Steve, had painted Psalm 23, a picture of a Shepherd with his sheep. "The Lord is my shepherd, there is nothing I shall want" demonstrates complete trust in the Lord. It is a painting I will always treasure. How interesting this stranger would come with what I have been praying for all along. When feeling helpless, I feel relief in giving my worry to the Lord and trusting in Him. I have to do this over and over.

My mother takes the children upstairs so we can give our full attention to this experience. Looking back, I'm sorry I didn't have them present to witness the beautiful prayers for Cathy Anne and our family. It had a calming effect on me.

I hand Cathy Anne, dressed in a pink sundress, slowly to Kevin, our special friend. Her little body fits snuggly into his hands like a puzzle. I am giving my child to another who will implore God to heal her.

Kevin begins the session by holding Cathy Anne's frail body.

"Dear God, we implore you to heal Cathy Anne and make her whole. May your will be done and help us accept the outcome whatever it may be. All for the greater honor and glory of God. Bless Cathy Anne's heart and make it strong and work the right way."

Her eyes, her ears, her brain, her chromosomes, and her whole body got special attention from him. Ellen and Steve and the other members also pray over her. This lasts about three hours. I notice Cathy Anne's breathing becomes slower and not so labored. I feel anxiety, my constant companion, lift right out of me. The care and comfort from loving friends doing God's work helps me. I can feel God's presence in the room.

Tonight, when the prayers are offered for Cathy Anne, I realize that my agony with Cathy Anne took me to an inner place I never experienced before, a place where God dwells and He holds me safely. This emotional crisis that interrupted my wonderful world, where life had been so perfect, had left me with a scary feeling of how I will be when Cathy Anne dies. Sitting with this, I am able to move through it and come out the other side with the feeling that I can handle anything in life after experiencing this. I feel empowered and at peace with whatever will happen to Cathy Anne.

When Cathy Anne has her weekly checkup, her pediatrician says,

"She looks better today than your last visit and her breathing is better."

I tell him about the prayer group. I know we will cope and be alright whatever happens to Cathy Anne. I am happy to hear his assessment of Cathy Anne. However, I remember the hospital pediatrician's words, "You can take her out, go to the picnic, but she can die at any time."

I have to sit with these uncomfortable feelings and continue to pray for strength.

CHAPTER 18

We feel like an ordinary family on an ordinary day

We are invited to only one event during Cathy Anne's lifetime at Lloyd Hall, home of some of the Christian Brothers in Riverdale, New York. It is a family picnic with John's colleagues at Manhattan College where John is an organic chemistry professor. My mother dresses Cathy Anne in her white sun suit while I help the children pick out play clothes. Most important to them are their new sneakers so they can run fast when they play hide and seek and climb enormous boulders. They each pick out jeans. Mary Christina chooses her favorite Wonder Woman t-shirt. Johnny decides on a black t-shirt with the Batman logo. If only Diana Prince and Bruce Wayne could come to save their day!

The grounds have spectacular trees with sweet smelling flowers. It has small cottages on the grounds that previously housed celebrities who were there for alcohol addiction where they were to dry out. The college purchased this land years ago. It is peaceful, a piece of heaven in harmony with nature, birds flying overhead to the various trees. The magnolia tree is magnificent with its perfumed, sweet fragranced pink flowers. Its canopy provides protection from the sun.

There is a building that has large rooms and a huge kitchen with a humongous refrigerator housing a variety of meat, drinks, fruit and vegetables. What a sight for the children to see. They are amazed at all the food there. We had been looking forward to this outing knowing the faculty are very special and understanding. We want to be with them to show off Cathy Anne especially since she did not have a baptismal party. It is nice to get out of the house and be with others.

"We're happy you could come so we can meet Cathy Anne," says Brother William who is Mary Christina's godfather.

"We're glad to be with friends," I say.

Brother William peers into Cathy Anne's carriage and says, "Glad to meet you, Cathy Anne. You are adorable."

We feel like an ordinary family on an ordinary day. When friends come to greet us, no one says anything about her ashen gray color or prognosis.

Audrey comes over. She looks into the carriage and says, "What a cute baby. Glad you could come."

Barbara and Joe come over. "Glad to meet you, Cathy Anne. We've heard so much about you. Welcome to the college family!"

Brother William sits down with us. "How are you doing?"

"Okay. I guess we're doing the best we can under these circumstances. We're happy to have her home." We sit and chat about Johnny and Mary Christina, the prayer groups and support we've received. We also discuss things going on at the college, new faculty, and reminisce about good times we've shared together.

Nanny stays with Cathy Anne while I go over to the children who are having lunch under the big magnolia tree.

Mary Christina and Johnny are sitting at a table with Megan, Mary Beth, and Anita who have been friends since birth, attending various family functions held here which we go to throughout the year. They are taking a break from their games so they can eat their hot dogs and hamburgers. Soda is also available which is a treat since Mary Christina and Johnny don't get it at home. To this day, the children, now young adults, still talk about their fun playing on the boulders, making beautiful memories they will always cherish.

My mother has accompanied us many times to the various functions at Lloyd Hall throughout the year. She considers the faculty members her friends. She is still struggling with the timing of her planned trip to Florida. She speaks about her dilemma with the faculty. They all encourage her to go. I know I am surrounded by good friends that are looking out for her best interests. My mother values what they have to say. They are caring and supportive. I know I will miss her, but I want her to have time to rest. I worry about her doing so many chores and not taking time for herself.

CHAPTER 19, AUGUST 16, 1977

Cathy Anne is dying ... and I am helpless

We are preparing for my mother's trip. We wish her bon voyage and everyone hugs and kisses her when she leaves. That day, Cathy Anne wakes up irritable and cries inconsolably all day, unusual for her so I hold her most of the day. The children take turns rocking her in her carriage. I didn't think much of this because I think she misses my mother.

"She looks awful. Listless. Her breathing is shallow," John exclaims when he comes home from work. "Oh, my goodness, John. I didn't see this all day!" At that very moment, the radio is on and the news is blaring that Elvis Presley died. When I hear the word *died*, it hits me—Cathy Anne is dying! An overwhelming sense of helplessness comes over me. I realize then I am the one missing my mother and Cathy Anne 's fussiness is a sign she is actively dying. What a shock! How could I have missed this? I call our pediatrician who offers help in the way of medication.

When I arrive at his office with Cathy Anne, he says, "Would you like to put Cathy Anne in the hospital?"

"No. I want her to die at home with us."

"Where's John?"

"He's home with the kids."

"I can give Cathy Anne an injection to calm her."

I shake my head up and down, "Yes."

He picks her up so gently and gives her the injection in her thigh, an anti-anxiety medication that he had ready for her.

"Is there anything I can do for you?"

"No, you've done everything. Thank you for the care you gave her so I can take her home now."

I appreciate his concern and that he offers me options. I want to get home quickly so John can see her before she dies. I don't think she has much time left. Her arms and legs are cold and her breathing is weak. Symptoms I didn't notice all day.

"She's close to dying?"

He shakes his head "Yes" in agreement.

I will always be grateful to him for his care, kindness, and support to us.

Cathy Anne is quiet on the ride home. I'm praying she will hold on until John can see her. We are fortunate the children are asleep. This gives John and me time to talk without having to focus on them.

When I arrive home, John says, "Take a picture of me with her."

We have a rocking chair in the middle of the hallway because of the renovations in the kitchen. My living room and dining room are cluttered with all the contents from the kitchen cabinets. John sits in the rocking chair. I hand Cathy Anne to him. She looks so comfortable in his arms as he rocks her. Her breathing is slower and slower. I take their picture. As I am taking the second picture, the film rolls up making a whirling sound. Cathy Anne takes her last breath. I go to her. I look at her. I don't see her breathing. I get closer and touch her. Her chest does not move.

I say, "Thank God she's dead, I couldn't do this another day."

Where did this come from? I can't believe I said that! We had been hop-ing she would live till Christmas. All I was feeling was relief. I could feel my shoulders relax. I was so afraid of how I would be when she died, but I'm fine, thank God.

John holds her and kisses her. We sit in silence for about ten minutes. I look at her in John's arms. I'm so thankful I got home before she died.

"I can't believe I was holding her when she died," says John.

"How was it for you?"

"It was life changing. Healing. I'm not afraid of death anymore. What a gift from Cathy Anne and God."

"What better place for a baby at time of death than in her father's arms, especially for you since you had such a fear of death. It was a comfort for me to see her in your arms."

"I was so worried she'd die before you got home."

"That's why I hurried."

"You did a fantastic job keeping the kids involved with Cathy Anne while I was at work."

"It was easier having her here. Thanks for agreeing to take her home. Her memories are treasures like gold. She was a contented baby. I'm gonna miss her."

"I'll miss holding her. I loved walking around the house with her. I loved her smell. She was beautiful."

"We did have our differences about her beauty," I laugh.

"How will the children be?" asks John.

"They'll handle it. Children do better than adults. I want the children to see her, so I'll wait till morning to call the funeral director."

While holding her, John says, "I enjoyed you every day, before I went to work and when I came home." He gives Cathy Anne a kiss. "Thanks, Cathy

Anne, for coming to live with us. We'll always love you. You're a special gift from God."

John hands Cathy Anne to me.

"Thanks for being in our family." I kiss her and say, "You're an angel sent by God who came to stay a little while. You'll always be part of our family. Ask God to take care of your siblings and us. Let's pray. Thank you, God, for giving us the strength and courage to take care of her at home. Thank you, God, for letting me get home. Seeing her die in John's arms was beautiful. We're grateful for the gift of Cathy Anne. Let's say the three Hail Mary's in thanksgiving for the life of Cathy Anne."

I hold her for about ten minutes. I don't want to put her down but kiss her on her cheeks then place her in the cradle. Johnny's Winnie-the-Pooh blanket is underneath her. I wrap it around her. She looks so peaceful. She doesn't need anything from us.

John gives me a kiss on my cheek, takes my hand and we go upstairs.

CHAPTER 20

Her brother began to paint rocks for her grave

I am able to sleep most of the night. I wake up a few times, realizing Cathy Anne is not with us. Her bassinet, next to my bed, is empty and she is downstairs in her cradle. She didn't need anything from me, so there's no need to bring her upstairs. Tonight is so different from every other night when she was alive. I miss her being next to me and sleeping so peacefully. I had hoped she would live until Christmas, which is still four months away. I don't know why I picked Christmas. But it is a time for celebrating with family.

My arms ache from missing her. My heart feels like a knife has pierced it, which leaves me with a very empty feeling mixed with a sense of relief. When she was alive, I was happy to take care of her, feed her, hold her, take walks with her, but I wondered how I'd be when she died. Now I know I will be okay. I wonder how I would have managed if she lived a long time. How do other parents manage with a sickly child? We were blessed to have her even for a short time. She is happy with God. We have an angel in heaven, but I would prefer to have her here with us without any difficulties.

When I wake up in the morning, many thoughts bombard my thinking. Cathy Anne is gone. I feel like I am missing a very important part of my life. Thank God she died in John's arms which helped him cope with death. It was a comfort to me that both of us were with her as she took her last breath. Then I think of the things she liked and seemed to enjoy, like her sponge baths, her walks in her carriage with Johnny and Mary Christina pushing her and cannot help but smile.

When the children wake up, they run into our bedroom.

"Where's Cathy Anne?" says Johnny, and looks at the empty bassinet.

"Cathy Anne died last night. She's downstairs in the living room."

"I wanna see her."

John and I go first. Johnny flies down the stairs with Mary Christina behind him. He goes over to her cradle, kneels, and pinches her. He wants to see what death is. Would the pinch make her move? She doesn't. He looks at her eyes. They are open.

"Her eyes should be closed," Johnny says.

I shake my head "Yes" so he closes them. Mary Christina just watches and holds my hand without saying anything.

Cathy Anne looks the same as she did when she was alive. Her color, an ashen gray when she was alive, looks the same in death. Now she does have a bluish tinge around her lips.

"Let's say a prayer." We all form a circle around Cathy Anne and hold hands. "Thank God we had Cathy Anne home so we could take care of her. We all took good care of her and did the best we could. Johnny and Mary Christina were the best big brother and sister. You shared your toys with her and held her and rocked her in her carriage." We all hug.

I call the funeral home and shortly afterwards the funeral director arrives. He picks up Cathy Anne and wraps her in the Winnie-the-Pooh blanket and places her in a box. It is a tiny shoe-like box, made of Styrofoam. When he is about to leave, Johnny starts to cry, "I want my Winnie-the Pooh blanket back."

"Please give the blanket to Johnny."

He is very gracious, opens the box and unwraps her little body.

Johnny says, "She should be in a white blanket and a white dress." He runs upstairs and comes down with the white blanket and white dress. The man carefully wraps her in the blanket and places the dress on top of her. It is comforting to see this man so compassionate and kind listen to the wishes of a little boy.

I explain to the children, "We are going to bury Cathy Anne tomorrow where my grandma and Aunt Anna are buried. These are two special family members I grew up with and Cathy Anne was named after."

"I want her buried in the backyard next to Snowball," says Johnny.

"I'm sorry. I can see why you would want Cathy Anne buried next to Snowball, but it's not allowed. It's against the board of health to bury people in your backyard. People are buried in a special place called a cemetery."

He doesn't say much more about this for now. He did begin painting rocks for her grave the same way he did for his cat, Snowball, when he died.

CHAPTER 21

Tears are running down my face and I can't stop them

John's family comes to the house in the morning. His parents are the first to arrive, followed by John's sister's family. As I'm making breakfast, my three-year-old niece is in the kitchen with me. I'm happy she and her siblings are here to be with our children. Tears are running down my face and I can't stop them. All I can think of is the fact that I have to get through this day. We won't have a funeral Mass because it is not necessary for a baby, which I regret. She didn't need it, but we could have benefited from it since a Mass is a traditional part of saying goodbye to a beloved family member.

I call my mother, who is in Florida. I don't see any point in her cutting her trip short. She was there for us when we needed her. I'm glad she is with friends at this sad time.

When we arrive at the cemetery, several friends are at the burial site. The funeral director places Cathy Anne at the grave. I wanted to see her one more time but didn't ask. I didn't mention it to anyone. I think people will think that's weird and I'm weird for wanting to open the casket to see my dead baby. I'm not one to worry about what people think, but in this situation, I feel some would be horrified to see a casket opened. People aren't comfortable with dead things. My thoughts bombard me. I wonder if they dressed her in her white dress and wrapped her in her white blanket Johnny picked out. There never could have been enough time for me with her. I think letting go of her was hard and seeing her once more wouldn't have changed anything—my missing her. The funeral is so final and there is no redo. Stuart, our parish priest, says prayers over her. After the prayers, as we are about to leave, Johnny begins to cry.

"What's the matter, Johnny?" says John.

"I want to see her put in the ground."

John goes over to the gravediggers, "Please lower her into the ground. Our son requested this." They are kind and lower her carefully into the grave.

That night Johnny says, "I wanted to see her put in the ground because I was afraid they might drop her." He uses his little hands to show how she should be placed gently into the ground. He helped take care of her when she was alive, and he wanted to be sure she was buried carefully. He also thought the cemetery was too far away but being there he thought it wasn't so far. We were fortunate Johnny's questions were answered and he felt good about decisions made for his little sister.

Unlike her big brother, Mary Christina just observed everything. She didn't have the words to express herself in the same manner that Johnny did. In the months that follow, Mary Christina would recall the events that John did as her own. I saw the effect of grief on the memory of my three-year old. For example, she recalled closing Cathy Anne's eyes when she died and asked the gravediggers to lower Cathy Anne into the ground.

When we arrive home from the burial, the phone rings.

"Hi! I'm Jim, a photographer. You filled out a request at the mall to take pictures of your newborn."

"I would have loved that, but she died."

"I'm sorry."

"It's too bad you didn't call sooner. We buried her today. We have two other children. Would you be able to take their picture instead?"

I would have loved to have a professional picture of Cathy Anne with Johnny and Mary Christina. He came a few weeks later and took our children's picture.

CHAPTER 22

Goodbye Mommy and Daddy, Johnny, Mary Christina and Nanny

I recall as long ago as the day Cathy Anne died and as recently as today, wondering what this little baby was feeling. What did she experience? Did she sense our presence? Was she aware of how much we loved her? And then I celebrate the gift of my own imagination and I translate those imaginings into what might have been Cathy Anne's own words. And so, I let her speak for herself.

I began my life with so much pain being pricked and prodded in the hospital. I never felt like I could catch my breath. I was always cold and afraid. But everything changed when I recognized mommy's soft voice from when I was in her tummy and daddy's gentle touch. Although many of my days are a blur, the most important memories I have are of the people who loved me.

I remember being in my mommy's warm arms, feeling the beat of her heart when I was cuddled close to her. I loved her massage and gentle care. She nourished me and I could feel her love.

I remember my daddy's protection. I felt safe to be in his arms. His soothing voice calmed me and he made me feel special. He helped me to be relaxed and comfortable so I could die.

I remember Nanny singing and rocking me. I can still hear the words "Lovely lady dressed in blue, teach me how to pray. God was just your little boy and you know the way." I felt her care and love every time she sang to me. Her prayers gave me hope.

I remember Johnny pushing me in the carriage and sharing his favorite toys. I felt so honored to be adored by my big brother. He always protected me.

I remember Mary Christina wind the little blue elephant and sing along with the tune, "You are My Sunshine." She made me feel special. I loved to be held gently in her little arms.

I hoped I would get better because I loved my family. But this was not what happened.

Everything faded. The world went away. I saw an angel with outstretched hands beckon to me. She looked friendly and smiled. I thought I should go to her. My soul could sink right into her arms. I felt safe and loved and happy. I guess I was in heaven or was on my way there. Goodbye Mommy and Daddy, Johnny, Mary Christina and Nanny. Thank you for all you did for me. I am at peace. I know I'm loved and safe in the arms of the angel.

CHAPTER 23

I never thought I would have a baby that would die

It has been a few days since Cathy Anne died. I'm thinking about her as I'm loading the dishwasher after dinner. A sadness comes over me as I feel my breasts fill with milk. Yet another reminder of Cathy Anne. I keep picturing Cathy Anne's little face with her feeding tube. I don't want to forget her features—her almond-shaped eyes, low-set ears, her brown hair. When she was first born, I thought these features were ugly but as I got to take care of her and to know and love her, I saw her as beautiful. Even her ashen color was pretty. I am grateful to God for being with me on Cathy Anne's final journey.

John stays home for two weeks after Cathy Anne's death. We go over special memories of taking her to the park and feeding her. Her weak little cry was precious. The day John goes back to work, I feel empty and alone. My heart is broken in half. My arms ache for her. I need to talk to someone, so I call Barbara from Le Leche League. The last time I spoke with her Cathy Anne was alive. I feel a connection to Barbara and appreciate her support. She made my life easier with Cathy Anne. When I felt alone without John and Cathy Anne, I thought to call her.

I thank Barbara for her generosity.

"I'm so sorry Cathy Anne died," Barbara says.

"Thank you. I appreciate the Gumco machine you gave me. It made it easy to express milk."

We make small talk for the next few minutes. I'm ready for the day.

A few days later, I go back to teaching one day a week at Pace University. My first day back, meeting faculty I hadn't seen since Cathy Anne's death is painful. I can hardly say anything, holding back tears, but they are kind and understanding. I wonder how I will do it in my class. These students don't know me, so there won't be any questions about Cathy Anne.

One student meets me outside the classroom before class.

"Hello, Mrs. Wasacz. I'm Steven. I know your class is closed but I need this class to graduate in January."

I say to myself, *what's one more student?*

"Sure, you can," I tell Steven.

I give the assignment to the class. They need to choose a relevant nursing issue. The next week when I look at Steven's topic, I am so angry. Why did I let him into my class? He could have chosen something that wasn't so controversial and close to home. I could kick myself. He chose to write a pro-abortion paper. I am not ready to look at this. I need more time.

Steven writes a well-written pro-abortion argument. Although I don't agree with his position, I'm glad I have the opportunity to have all the research available. Perhaps it is good Steven came with this topic and I am well-informed now. I am confident in my decision to possibly go forward in another pregnancy even though there are risks. I still would not have an abortion.

Later that night I realize another decision must be made about the Lamaze class I teach. I wish I hadn't scheduled a class, but I never thought I would have a baby that would die. I thought my baby was going to be healthy.

"John, how can I look at all those pregnant women in my Lamaze class? It is painful to see them with their impending births, having experienced such loss."

"Well, you could sit in on one of your colleague's classes before your class begins or you can wait a while before starting again."

"You always have such good ideas."

I pick up the phone and ask Sigrid, a Lamaze instructor, if I can observe her class before teaching my class again.

"Sure, you can," Sigrid says.

I have a four-hour break from Pace's class before Sigrid's class in her home in Briarcliff.

When my class is finished, I head over to see where she lives. I drive through Briarcliff with its winding roads and beautiful greenery, and think about Cathy Anne with no interruptions. With every thought there are tears. It sinks in that I will never hold her again. I think of bathing her, feeding her, rocking her. She is in heaven and I will see her someday. How I wish she were here with me and healthy.

How can I sit through Sigrid's class without crying? I pray and put myself in God's hands that He will be with me and get me through. I do this drive several times to become acquainted with the route, waste time, and to think about Cathy Anne.

There are only two couples at Sigrid's when I arrive, which I am thankful for. I can ease into this. I take a seat in the back. I don't have any desire to talk with them and no one approaches me.

Eight more couples complete the class. Sigrid introduces me as a Lamaze teacher observing her class. I'm okay so far. Seeing those happy couples, I hope they each have a healthy baby. I pray for them.

It is dark driving home from Sigrid's, but my dry run makes me confident. It was not horrible being in class with pregnant women. I am not tearful driving home. I'm ready to have my scheduled Lamaze class four weeks from now. This is a big achievement for me.

CHAPTER 24

*I will keep you in my prayers. When
would you like me to call again?*

John sees an announcement for a conference at Downstate Medical Center
on Perinatal Loss scheduled for October, 1977. I search bookstores and
the library but find only one book that has a few pages devoted to perinatal
loss. I am thrilled about this conference and decide to attend. I want to learn
more about newborn loss. I realize how difficult it is to find out anything
about this topic and this will be a good place to start.

The conference has speakers who are professional experts on miscarriage, stillbirth and neonatal death. About seventy people are waiting in the
audience for a panel of four couples to present their experience on the death
of their newborns. No one on the panel shows. I raise my hand and speak
about my experience at the hospital Cathy Anne was transferred to and the
excellent care we received. Afterwards, Paula, a supervisor on the NICU
at Cathy Anne's hospital comes over to me and we set up an appointment
for me to meet her at the hospital to have a role volunteering with neonatal
death. Several days later I meet with her and the head of the NICU, who was
Cathy Anne's doctor.

"You could have a hotline in your home," he says. "Paula will call with the name of the family whose baby died. You can call them and assess how they are doing."

One of the first people I call is Susie, whose second baby was stillborn. I introduce myself and offer condolences.

"My heart goes out to you," I say. "Did you name your baby?"

"Joseph, after my father-in-law."

"What happened to your baby, Joseph?"

"Joseph was very active throughout my pregnancy. When I woke up on Tuesday, he was quiet. I thought he was sleeping. By two o'clock, I couldn't feel any movement. I called my obstetrician who said to come in. My husband came with me. The doctor couldn't hear a heartbeat. Three days later, I went into labor. He came out four hours later. The cord was around his neck," Susie says as she blows her nose.

"How did you manage to cope while waiting to go into labor?"

"My husband, Steven, was with me all the time. He was my rock. My two-year-old, Robby, needed attention. My mother came to play with him."

"Did you get to see Joseph?"

"No. The nurse took him from the room right away. I don't know what he looked like. I don't know if he looked like my other son, Robby. I never got to hold him. It was like going to a play and never seeing the ending. I buried him with my Aunt Josie. That was comforting. I felt like a robot. I was just going through the motions. I was in a daze. I did what anybody told me. I wish I had seen him but didn't know what to do."

"You can look at your picture of Robby as a newborn and think of Joseph looking like his brother. Then you have an image of Joseph you can remember. What is helping you now?"

"My family. When Steven went back to work, my sister, Nancy came up each day. Now, I'm okay being alone. I'm thankful I have Robby. I never imagined my baby could die."

"Do you have a particular faith?"

"Yes, Catholic, but I feel so angry at God. I can't pray. How could this have happened to me? I'm a good person. I ate healthy food, and did everything I was supposed to do."

"It's hard to understand how this happened. Your baby dying has nothing to do with being a good person. Your anger at God is your prayer right now. Your family and friends can pray for you when you can't. I will keep you and your family in my prayers. When would you like me to call again?"

"Next week."

CHAPTER 25

This bereavement group will provide Cathy Anne's purpose for me

R ita E. Watson from The New York Times interviews John and me over
the phone for the Sunday, January 14, 1979 article entitled, 'A Hotline
of Solace for Bereaved Parents.'

As a result, three women call. They talk about the death of their newborns and how hard it is for them. I ask if they would like to meet with other parents whose baby died? "Oh, yes," was their immediate response. The fathers were not interested in coming.

The following week, the Infant Bereavement Group is formed. The meeting is in the daytime in my home and lasts an hour and a half. I arrange the chairs in circle with a box of Kleenex on the table. I feel well-prepared to lead this group.

I am thrilled this group is taking place because there was nothing available for perinatal loss in Westchester County, New York and there is a great need for parents to have a place to talk about their baby. From the time Cathy Anne was born and didn't breathe, I felt God sent her for a purpose. Why waste all this pain without doing something beneficial for others? This bereavement group will provide Cathy Anne's purpose for me. I know God is walking with me.

I have attended conferences on perinatal loss at Downstate Medical Center, workshops on grief at Immaculate Heart of Mary, where I was part of the panel on loss, and a course at Manhattan College, Death as a Fact of Life, and continue with the hotline at the hospital. I am also a clinical nurse specialist in adult psychiatric—mental health, certified by the American Nurses Association. I have much to offer the group which makes me feel confident. I ask God's blessing.

"Please God let this group work for these families," I pray. "Help me find the right words to say to each one and that they will find the group helpful. Please be with each one in their sorrow. Thanks."

The first to arrive is Rachael, a petite woman with big blue eyes and blonde hair whose baby died eight weeks ago. She holds her scarf tightly as she fingers it.

Ellen is a tall statuesque woman with dark hair whose baby was born a year ago and lived a few hours. She never saw her baby. She turns her wedding band as she talks.

Julie is a stocky brown-eyed, black-haired woman whose baby was born six months ago and lived three months before dying of Sudden Infant Death Syndrome. She is soft-spoken and fidgets with the pendant around her neck.

I open the session, saying, "You're all brave to come here to talk about your babies. I can see the pain on your faces. My heart goes out to you. Who would like to begin?"

Rachael has tears in her eyes as she says, "My baby weighed two pounds and lived for three days. I never held him." She sobs. "He looked scary with tubes all over. I couldn't even touch him. In the Jewish religion, the baby isn't recognized if he only lived a short time," she says while tears continue to run down her face.

I offer her a tissue and validate her thoughts by saying, "It's important for you to mourn your baby, even though he was tiny. He was your baby. The reason babies weren't always mourned was because it was common for newborns to die."

Rachael became animated saying, "I'm angry that the rabbi told me, 'You're young, you can have more children.' because I want this one."

"Of course, you do," I say. "Having another baby wouldn't take away the pain. People don't know what to say to comfort you."

How fortunate I was to have Cathy Anne at home for three weeks, to hold her and to see her as beautiful as I got to know and love her. My heart goes out to Rachael. I remember being in her place with deep suffering.

Each mother in the group shares freely and is supportive of each other. They came in tearful but were able to leave smiling at one another. Much love and compassion are evident and will continue next week.

CHAPTER 26

I pray, which we do daily, and every time
I think of having another baby

It's been six months since Cathy Anne died and I think about having another baby. Although the thought is scary, I think my desire to have another child is beginning to overtake my fear of the next baby dying.

"John, remember sitting in the small cream-colored room with the cardiac surgeon who gave us Cathy Anne's diagnosis?"

"I sure do. That scene is imprinted on my brain. There's a one in 80 chance it could happen again."

"Remember telling the obstetrician when I went for a checkup and he said, "Pretty good odds at the racetrack""

John shakes his head "Yes" in agreement.

"John, life is filled with risks. Remember the time you were on a bus and there was a man with a gun? You could have been killed. The lady crossing the street down the block was hit by a car."

"Do you think it's worth the risk?" asks John.

"I do. We did everything humanly possible to give Cathy Anne a good and meaningful life. She gave us so much being home with us so the children could also be part of her life. I think this is what is helping me heal. Luckily, we were able to reach out to other parents suffering the loss of their babies. Why have all this pain and not do something to help another parent?"

"Yeah, I got lots of phone calls. You were out."

"You were so good with the parents."

"My fear of having another baby with Trisomy 18 is very real. Since it happened once, it could happen again," says John.

"You're right, it could, but we don't know if it would. I keep asking God to help me in this decision. My age is another factor, so if we want another baby, we need to act soon because the chances for a recurrence increase with age."

"I enjoyed Cathy Anne so much," John tells me. "She was a delight. I feel privileged to have gotten to know her. She helped me deal with death, which was so frightening for me. I learned to drive, another fear I had, but figured if she could go through all her suffering, I could learn to drive. And I did. Thanks for wanting to take her home."

It was true. John didn't drive before but got his license so he'd be available to take us to the doctor or hospital whenever we needed to go.

"My thinking is beginning to shift. We coped with her diagnosis, and we would cope if it happened again. We have to storm the heavens for a healthy baby," says John.

"Dear God please help us with our decision," I pray, which we do daily, and every time I think of having another baby. After several days talking about this, we decided we could have another baby and are overjoyed when the pregnancy is eventually confirmed. Being pregnant is hard but trusting in God helps.

Pregnancy under normal conditions has its ups and downs with all those hormones floating around. When the pregnancy follows a baby that has died, there is added upheaval. My anxiety rises from time to time leaving me on a roller coaster and prayer helps settle me down with something I have no control over. John is a wonderful support when my anxiety increases, assuring me we will cope with whatever happens.

"Will this pregnancy end with a healthy baby?" I ask God to help me with my questions.

I would not have an abortion so there is no need to risk an amniocentesis. There is so much I have no control over in life and putting myself in God's hands that He will help me is all I can do. I know that letting go and letting God will get me through this pregnancy and help me cope whatever the outcome, but I will be devastated beyond belief if I don't have a healthy baby.

John and I attend a healing workshop at Immaculate Heart of Mary Church. I meet a nun whom I tell about Cathy Anne and that I am pregnant. She gives me a relic of St. Elizabeth Anne Seton, foundress of the Sisters of Charity. She said she would keep this baby and us in her prayers, giving me comfort. John and I agree if this baby is a girl, she will be named Elizabeth Anne, after the saint.

"How many children do you have?" a parishioner at the workshop asks.

Such an innocent question but not so easy when one of your children died. Do I include Cathy Anne? She is my child, but in heaven. I have to think about this question, so I abruptly excuse myself. The next day this question is asked again.

While shopping at a local children's store in Scarsdale, I pick up brown dress slacks for Johnny and as I'm reaching for a blue dress off the rack for Mary Christina, a young woman passes by and asks, "How many children do you have?"

Again, I question what should I say? Finally, I say, "I have three children."

Later another woman. shopping in the same store asks the question and I say, "I have two children."

The first woman now at the register says, "You said you have three children before. Did you lose track of your children?"

It is then I realize that I don't have to tell strangers about Cathy Anne.

On good days I feel positive. Dark days I fear another Trisomy 18 baby. Prayer and trust in God help me in day-to-day living. Today is a rough day for me. I see baby shoes in a closet so I decide to give them away saying to the baby, "If you're healthy, I'll buy you new shoes." Somehow getting rid of those shoes and the thought of buying new ones for my healthy baby helps me feel better. I had control over whether to keep the shoes or not. I have no control over the health of my baby, except to do the right things for him or her.

That evening I am on a panel at Immaculate Heart of Mary, Coping with Loss. In the audience is a nun who suggests I picture my baby healthy three times a day in an outfit that helps me bond with this baby. A friend gives me the outfit I had pictured the baby in. While here I learn of the prayer group at Immaculate Heart of Mary.

I go to the prayer group alone three weeks later. The time comes for people to ask for what they need. I can't. I'm crying so I ask my neighbor to ask for me. What comes to my mind is, "Ask and you shall receive," as it says in the Bible. I know I have to ask. I am finally able through tears to ask for a healthy baby.

When I come home, I sigh as I say to John, "It was so sad and hard trying to ask for a healthy baby, but I did it and feel much better."

"Glad you were able," he tells me.

"I feel it was very healing for me. Several people from the prayer group came over to me after the service and prayed over me. I felt that God is listening to my heart and my desire for another healthy baby."

I see God manifest Himself through people here on earth. God is helping me every day by the people He sends into my life, which makes me feel blessed.

John sets up the crib for the new baby. A friend has clothes for our new baby, but I told her to hold onto them until the baby is born. I have several clothing items that I pack in a bag to take to the hospital. A friend knitted a bunting for the baby which I pack. It is November 10 and the baby is due November 26. John puts the car seat in the car. I am ready for our new baby. My pregnancy was easy, physically—no problem except for the pain in my legs, alleviated by the Jobst stockings which I wore during my previous pregnancies. I enjoy being pregnant and have my days of enjoyment mixed with fear if this baby will be healthy. Prayer helps.

Finally, the day comes when I go into labor. My previous labors were easy. Today my water broke so I go to the hospital and have an IV with Pitocin administered which makes the contractions much stronger. I have oxygen running. I cope okay until a student comes in and tells me I am having a difficult labor, but it never occurs to me I am having problems. My contractions were well controlled until I got this information. This is the longest labor I have—twelve hours in the hospital. The contractions are uncontrollable.

All I can think is that I'm going to burn my Lamaze charts. This isn't working and after this labor, will my baby be healthy? Prayer helps. I know God is walking with me, and I'm grateful.

Finally, our baby arrives.

A little pink baby boy who lets out a robust cry!

What a beautiful color he has. Such a contrast to Cathy Anne's ashen gray. How happy we are. We name him Anthony, after St. Anthony. Life is good. God has given us the gift of faith that He will take care of us and our children.

EPILOGUE

Helping all my children, helped me

Cathy Anne taught me many things in her brief life. From the moment she was born and didn't breathe, I learn patience and how to sit with the unknown, with something I have no control over. God walked with me these painful days and held me safely. I trust in Him and know I can handle anything that happens in my life because of Cathy Anne.

"Cathy Anne, you sure knew how to rip the heart out of a person, but in the end, you put one back in me that was much bigger and better than I could have ever imagined. You turned my world upside down. Thanks for coming into our family and sharing your life with us. We will always remember and love you."

ACKNOWLEDGMENTS

On the amazing journey, my family took with our third child, Cathy Anne, I am awed by the people who played a role to inspire, support and guide us, and those who are helping me write about it today.

I wish to thank the doctors for their support and medical expertise in helping us understand Cathy Anne's condition and their support in taking her home.

Barbara and Joe Reynolds and Patti Plowden for their friendship.

Sonja Cooper who gave me strategies to enhance Cathy Anne's life.

Ellen and Kevin Moore who came with the Prayer Group to pray for Cathy Anne and our family. They gave unwavering support through prayer and friendship.

Msgr. Edwin Connors and Fr. Stuart Sandberg who consoled and prayed with us. They counseled us in difficult decision-making for Cathy Anne.

Jimin Han who was my instructor the first year in the Scarsdale Writer's Circle.

Barbara Josselsohn from the Scarsdale Writer's Circle who helped me develop my manuscript. Her patience and comforting ways in giving comments for improvement were greatly appreciated.

The Writer's Circle class critiqued my work in a very supportive and caring manner.

Ann Cefola, my mentor, who read my work and gave suggestions.

Marcia Bradley who edited my book in a very respectful way, making sure I was comfortable with her suggestions.

Family and friends too many to mention.

Kitty Perry, my mother, who helped with Cathy Anne's care daily and gave love to our family.

To my children, Johnny and Mary Christina, who loved their baby sister and played with her. Helping them, helped me.

Mary Christina for reading my manuscript and making suggestions.

Anthony, our fourth child, who helped me with computer problems in a loving and compassionate manner.

John Wasacz, my husband, the most important person in my life who shared this journey, helping me every step of the way. This is our story.

God who walked with me and gave me strength and courage.

ENDORSEMENTS

"This is an inspiring story about the life of Cathy Anne. It feels as if the reader goes through the experience with the author as the events unfold. It is an honest reaction to the tremendous difficulties and heartbreak involved in losing a newborn."

- Katherine B. Guerin Ph.D.

"This book radiates how Mary's Catholic faith as well as the support she receives from family and friends, turns their tragic experience into one in which Mary can say, "Life is good. God is with us and has given us the gift of faith that He will take care of us and our children."

- Thomas Mcgowan, Ph.D, Professor Emeritus
of religious studies, Manhattan College.
Marrianne Mcgowan, literary specialist
staff development, Westchester public schools.

2 REVIEWS

This is an unflinchingly honest account of how Mary Wasacz and her family coped when her third baby was born with a limited lifespan. While there is no fairytale ending, this is an uplifting story where Mary and her husband eventually find peace in pioneering a safe place where other bereaved parents can grieve.

Lucy Iscaro

A story of faith, hope and love that's engaging and heartfelt. A true account of a remarkable and daring decision that a family made to take a dying infant home at a time where it was unheard of.

Ann Foley